YAHWEH VERSUS BAAL:

A Conflict

of Religious Cultures

Yahweh versus Baal:
A CONFLICT OF RELIGIOUS CULTURES

A STUDY IN THE RELEVANCE OF
UGARITIC MATERIALS FOR
THE EARLY FAITH OF ISRAEL

by

NORMAN C. HABEL

WIPF & STOCK · Eugene, Oregon

Wipf and Stock Publishers
199 W 8th Ave, Suite 3
Eugene, OR 97401

Yahweh Versus Baal
A Conflict of Religious Culture
By Habel, Norman C.

ISBN 13: 978-1-5326-6277-5
Publication date 7/9/2018
Previously published by Bookman Associates, 1964

FOREWORD

THE NEED FOR AN EXAMINATION OF UGARITIC MATERIALS for their relevance to the early faith of Israel has been met by Norman C. Habel in a dissertation written for his Doctor of Theology degree from the School for Graduate Studies, Concordia Seminary, St. Louis. By revising and shortening his dissertation the author has put it into such a form that it can be printed and thus made available to a larger circle of scholars.

The descendants of Abraham, the chosen people of Yahweh, were bound to come into conflict with their neighbors. The strong emphasis on religion among all these peoples, particularly among the Israelites, would lead to a clash of religious cultures. A study of that conflict, reconstructed from the Ugaritic literary remains—which tell of only one aspect of the wider conflict—contributes to a better understanding of the premonarchic period of Israel's religious history. It sharpens the unique aspects of the covenant emphasis in the relationship between Israel and Yahweh.

Admittedly the author makes conjectures and advances plausibilities on the basis of the evidence before him. The historian in reconstructing the past, particularly when the records are fragmentary and incomplete, must use his "imagination" to determine the full scope of those records and their interrelationships. In doing this he does not forfeit the right to be heard, but creatively brings out the meaning of the past and gives significant insights into the culture of a period.

Professor Habel's scholarly comparison and contrast of the nature mysticism of the Canaanites and the faith of the Hebrew people demonstrates not only his mastery of the primary sources and the secondary literature of the period, but he brings together these materials, organizes them in a splendid fashion, and presents them in a cumulative manner. For this service the School for Graduate Studies commends this sixth volume in its series of publications.

CARL S. MEYER, *Director*
School for Graduate Studies
Concordia Seminary, St. Louis

25 September 1963

CONTENTS

SIGLA FOR THE TRANSLITERATION OF HEBREW AND UGARITIC 9

INTRODUCTION 11

I. THE CONFLICT TRADITION IN THE COVENANT FAITH OF ISRAEL 13
The Sinaitic Covenant Tradition, *13*
The Essential Content of the Sinaitic Covenant, *16*
The Covenant Renewal at Sinai, *20*
The Incident at Beth-Peor, *24*
The Crisis at Shechem, *27*

II. THE FAITH OF ISRAEL IN THE EARLY POETIC TRADITIONS 39
The Warrior King and His Mighty Feats, *40*
The Sovereign Lord and His Chosen One, *41*
The Covenant God and His Jealous Love, *44*

III. THE KINGSHIP OF BAAL AND THE KINGSHIP OF YAHWEH 51
The Purpose and Nature of the Ugaritic Kingship Texts, *51*
Baal's Decisive Battle for Kingship, *52*
The Exaltation of Baal as the Cosmic Overlord, *55*
The Kingship of Yahweh in "The Song of the Sea," *58*
The Relevance of the Battle for Kingship Motif, *62*

IV. THE THEOPHANY OF BAAL AND THE THEOPHANY OF YAHWEH 73
The Character of Baal as the Storm God, *73*
The Theophany of Baal from his Temple, *75*
The Temple Cultus of Baal as Storm God, *78*
The Theophanies of Yahweh in the Early Israelite Poetry, *80*
Yahweh's Theophany from His Temple, *84*
Psalm 29: Yahweh's Expression of Divine Kingship in a Storm Theophany, *86*

v. BAAL AS THE GOD OF FERTILITY AND YAHWEH AS THE GOD OF LIFE 93
The Descent of Baal to the Underworld of Mot, *93*
Mortuary Rites for Baal, *97*
The Harvesting of Mot and the Revivification of Baal, *98*
Drought and the Sympathy of Nature in the Old Testament, *101*
Agricultural Rituals in Israelite Society, *103*
Yahweh as the Lord of Life, *106*

GENERAL CONCLUSIONS 115

SELECTED BIBLIOGRAPHY 119

INDEX 123

SIGLA FOR THE TRANSLITERATION OF HEBREW AND UGARITIC

UGARITIC	HEBREW	SYMBOL
𐎀	א	’a
𐎛	א	’i
𐎜	א	’u
𐎁	ב	b
𐎂	ג	g
𐎄	ד	d
𐎏		ḏ
𐎅	ה	h
𐎆	ו	w
𐎇	ז	z
𐎈	ח	ḥ
𐎃		ḫ
𐎉	ט	ṭ
𐎑		ẓ
𐎊	י	y
𐎋	כ	k
𐎍	ל	l
𐎎	מ	m
𐎐	נ	n
𐎒	ס	s
𐎝		s̮
𐎓	ע	‘

UGARITIC	HEBREW	SYMBOL
𐎙		ǧ
𐎔	פּ	p
𐎕	צ	ṣ
𐎖	ק	q
𐎗	ר	r
	שׂ	ś
𐎌	שׁ	š
𐎚	ת	t
𐎘		ŧ
Long vowels		ā
		ī
		ū
Short vowels		a
		i
		u
Indistinct vowels		ạ
		ẹ
		ọ

INTRODUCTION

SINCE 1929 SCHOLARS HAVE BEEN CONCERNED WITH THE interpretation of certain Canaanite literary materials found at Ras Shamra in North Syria. The site of the discovery was known as Ugarit in ancient times. The Canaanite dialect spoken by its inhabitants has been designated Ugaritic. The attention of the scholarly world has also been drawn to a number of linguistic and cultural parallels between this corpus of literature and sections of the biblical record. But despite the numerous treatments of isolated points of contact between Ugaritic and biblical thought, one major question has not yet received an adequate answer. How and to what extent are the Ugaritic texts relevant for an appreciation of the fundamentals of the Israelite religion? It is the purpose of this study to answer at least part of this question by considering the major religious beliefs of Israel from the premonarchic period in the light of the Canaanite materials from Ugarit.

The immediate goal of the present analysis is to define the relevance of the Canaanite religious culture for an understanding of the early faith of Israel. In the first chapter the presence and prominence of certain early conflicts between the Israelite religion and its cultural environment will be demonstrated and the significance of these conflicts for an understanding of the covenant faith of Israel will be discussed. In the course of the chapter the essentials of Israel's covenant faith will be defined on the basis of Exod. 19:3-8. No attempt will be made at this point to determine the precise date of all the literary materials which incorporate these conflict traditions or the various covenant pericopes.

In Chapter Two, however, it will be shown that the same fundemental beliefs of this covenant faith are prominent in those poetic materials of Scripture which, according to recent scholarship, are demonstrably archaic. This archaic poetry will provide the major biblical source material for comparison with the Canaanite literature.

Specific religious patterns, imagery, concepts, terminology, and practices from Canaanite usage will be treated in Chapters Three through Five and the nature of their relationship with comparable biblical thought and practice will be analyzed. In so doing the essentials of Israel's covenant faith will also become more sharply defined and the antiquity of the conflict tradition more strongly affirmed.

In Chapter Three a comparison of the respective concepts of divine kingship in the Baal myth and in Exod. 15:1-18 leads to a deeper understanding of the *magnalia* of Yahweh's saving activities. In Chapter Four a consideration of Baal's self-disclosure in the storm and of Yahweh's theophanic self-revelations accentuates the sovereignty of Yahweh. And in Chapter Five a comparative analysis of Baal's role as the god of fertility and of Yahweh as the God over nature underscores the avid jealousy of Israel's God.

In brief the major thesis of the present work is that any interpretation of the premonarchic faith of Israel must take into consideration the conflict between the religious culture of Israel and that of its historical environment. The Ugaritic materials, in particular, are relevant to an understanding of the conflict between the religious cultures of Israel and Canaan, for an appreciation of the distinctive features of Israel's covenant faith and for a clarification of those areas where Canaanite religious influences are thought to be present in the biblical record.[1]

NOTE

[1] Suitable transliterations of the Ugaritic texts appear in C. Gordon, *Ugaritic Manual* (Rome: The Pontifical Biblical Institute, 1955), and in G. R. Driver, *Canaanite Myths and Legends* (Edinburgh: T. & T. Clark, 1956). The textual nomenclature and numbering of the latter will be followed in this work. Note that Baal I and Baal I* are separate texts, as are Baal III and Baal III.* Quotations from the Bible reflect the writer's own translation of the Hebrew original. Wherever possible, however, the wording of the Revised Standard Version has been favored. See *The Holy Bible* (New York: Thomas Nelson and Sons, 1952).

Chapter I

THE CONFLICT TRADITION IN THE COVENANT FAITH OF ISRAEL

One of the maxims of history might be designated "the law of reciprocity," that is, the action and interaction of culture with culture, the conscious and unconscious communication of traditions and ideals or the penetration and repulsion of religious forms and mores. In the early traditions of Israel one aspect of that law seems to be emphasized—the recurrent motif of a conflict between the faith of the jealous God of Israel and the religious culture of Israel's environment. The immediate objective of this chapter is to survey briefly this conflict in relation to the critical events of the early history of Israel and to indicate the relevance of this tradition for an appreciation of the essentials of the early faith of Israel.

The covenant is fundamental to the faith of Israel. Early covenant situations, therefore, should prove pertinent for an understanding of the critical moments in Israel's life. In these situations we may expect to find a specific religious conflict, a significant religious reaction, or a conscious religious polemic. At times the biblical record may even represent such conflict as a battle of the gods and covenant commitment as the Israelite's acknowledgement of the Victor.

The Sinaitic Covenant Tradition[1]

The persistent conviction that Yahweh hails from the South is a bold testimony to its own authenticity. Thus the ancient oracles acclaim Yahweh as "the One from Sinai" (Judg. 5:5) and as the "dawn" of Israel which rose from the mountains of the South (Deut. 33:2; cf. Hab. 3:3), and His advent in Israel's humiliating history as a theophany. Such a demand stands in direct antithesis to the Canaanite mythology in which the holy ones of a multifarious pantheon abide upon the heights of Ṣapon.[2] Sinai was sanctified by a moment in time; Ṣapon was the timeless residence of the Baal myth.

The biblical materials which form a prelude to the Sinai covenant include the various plague cycles, the crossing of the Reed Sea, the initial trials of the wilderness and the reunion with Jethro. Throughout this prelude the conflict motif persists. From the theological perspective of the biblical account one observes more than the rebellion of disgruntled Habiru or a mere trek of semi-nomads (if such there were) from one locale to another. There is a battle on a higher level. First, it is Yahweh versus Pharoah; ultimately it is Yahweh contending with the gods of Egypt. One plague follows another as the tension mounts, and each plague becomes an ominous act of Yahweh (*mōpēt*), a sign (*'ōt*), a glorious deed of judgment (*šepeṭ*).[3] Or as the climactic words of the passover memorial read: "On all the gods of Egypt I will execute judgment; I am Yahweh" (Exod. 12:12). It is this same Yahweh, who in jealousy for His name, also interferes to rescue and protect. For the victory is on behalf of Israel, over whom He will stand guard (*psḥ*), and as a witness against Egypt, over whom the Destroyer passes (*'br*) to vindicate the Name (Exod. 12:21-28).[4]

The immediate issue between Moses and Pharaoh is the right to celebrate a certain feast in the desert. The real question, however, is one of authority. The Egyptian magicians represent the power of Egyptian deities, while Moses strikes in the name of Yahweh.[5] It is unnecessary to equate each of the plagues with a specific polemic against a particular Egyptian god, as some have done. The situation is clear as it stands; Israel must behold the absolute victory of Yahweh so that its belief might be without reserve (Exod. 14:30f.). The humiliation of Pharaoh and the Egyptians must be complete (Exod. 12:36; 14:28) as Yahweh vindicates His supremacy (Exod. 14:4). The revolt of the Israelite tribes in Egypt is presented as something more than a political issue. It coincides with the conflict of the God of the Fathers and results in a religious experience of victory and release for the Israelites involved. (Ex. 3:13ff; 6:2ff).

Once the spectacular excitement of the exodus triumph dies, the struggle demands a more intimate and personal involvement on Israel's part. The child "Israel" is now on trial (Exod. 15:25). The conflict is still Yahweh versus Egypt, but the choice is now one of faith. For every rumble of discontent is tantamount to a breach of faith which makes the offender liable to the same fate as that of the Egyptians (Exod. 15:26). Whether the need of the hour is simply one of bread or water the "murmur" motif predominates.[6] It is a question of returning to the "fleshpots of Egypt" or of seeing "the glory of the Lord" (Exod. 16:3,7), and in the final analysis it is a question of whether "Yahweh is among us or not" (Exod. 17:7). In the jeopardy of present need Israel was often tempted to look back to "the good old days" and to the gods who had apparently blessed Egypt so bountifully.

The response of the Midianite priest Jethro stands in contrast to the wavering convictions of the Israelites. As far as he is concerned the conflict is resolved. "Now I know that Yahweh is greater than all other gods," he cries (Exod. 18:11). For the moment the pantheon of Egypt and the gods of Midian are displaced, and this moment provides the setting for the Sinai covenant. But as the ominous remark at the end of the covenant code indicates, a conflict between the gods of Canaan and the God of the Fathers was the heritage of each of the Israelite tribes in Canaan (Ex. 23:23f.).

These ancient conflict traditions which underlie the present biblical account are relevant for an understanding of the covenant formulations and the attendant legislations, even if these materials have been colored somewhat by reformulation in subsequent eras. The Sinai covenant was not born at an arbitrary moment of time, but in an hour of contention. It is the victory pledge of Yahweh the King.

The apodictic demands of the decalogue and the covenant code bear a distinctive character.[7] In the latter many of these demands are presented from a cultic and religious perspective while the religious emphasis[8] of the first five "words" of the former sets the tone for the ten "words" as a whole. The apodictic word is the categorical demand of the victorious King. Here, there is no room for casuistry, for "I Yahweh your God am a jealous God" as the theological comment on the first "word" asserts (Ex. 20:5). "No other gods besides me" is the necessary complement of the absolute "Thou shalt not. . . ." from a God who would humiliate every rival and disdain an image of Himself as much as He would of any of His created worlds (Exod. 20:3-5). Such words by themselves do not explicitly affirm or deny the existence and living reality of other gods than Yahweh, but they do suggest the potential claim, at least in the mind of the Israelite, of those so-called gods and powers with whom Yahweh must contend. Such gods, by the very temptations which they effect, become a reality for Israel and thereby evoke this apodictic demand from Yahweh as the suzerain. In a word, apodictic law is thoroughly consistent with the conflict tradition and points to its authentic and archaic character. In such a conflict there could be no compromise; no rival deities could be tolerated.[9]

The Essential Content of the Sinaitic Covenant

Against the background of the foregoing "conflict" tradition, the essential content of the Sinai covenant pericope (Ex. 19:3-6)[10] can be delineated. These essentials from the early covenant consciousness of Israel will provide a suitable outline with which to compare the basic propositions of the Canaanite religion of Palestine. The details of this comparison are the burden of later chapters of this work.

(a) The Witness Impact. "You, you have seen. . . ." is the initial thrust of this election formula.[11] The "House of Jacob" is Yahweh's witness. Something happened within the confines of history and time that was different; it was not the mock encounter of a familiar ritual. From the beginning Israel's faith rested upon a given historical act as the foundation of its grace relationship with Yahweh.[12] The impact of this primal act left an indelible imprint upon the heritage of "the sons of Israel" for, according to the refrain of Deuteronomy, "your own eyes have seen" the marvelous deeds of the Lord.[13] The persistence of this theme is in itself a testimony against the suggestion that these events are the historicization of some myth. Accordingly, the great conflict and victory of Yahweh is not merely a matter of record; it is, first of all, a question of personal historical involvement on the part of Israelite tribes.

As is well known, a witness motif is common to many ancient Near Eastern covenants and treaties. However, the witness concept in the pericope under discussion differs significantly from that of its pagan counterparts. Here Israel itself is witness while in the Hittite treaties the various cosmic gods and deified forms of nature testify to the conditions of the pact.[14] This difference is pertinent inasmuch as it highlights the impact of Israel's revelation consciousness and the irrelevance of any other god or power for the faith of the people of God. There is no other court of appeal for Israel. Or as Joshua later remarks, "you are witnesses against yourselves that you have chosen the Lord to serve Him" (Josh. 24:22). For what Israel had seen was its own salvation. Such a witness is in obvious antithesis to the mythological faith of Israel's neighbor's.

(b) The *Magnalia* of Yahweh. "What I did to Egypt" is the "saving word" for Israel. This word reproduces the import of Yahweh's victorious conflict with Egypt and the entire exodus operation with all its attendant glory. Egypt represents great world might and authority, the symbol of exalted gods and men. But Egypt is also a name written in the annals of history and not merely a creature of chaos or a perennial adversary of nature. In a word, Egypt in that day was the foe *par excellence*.[15] Hence the characteristic identification formula of Yahweh reads, "I am Yahweh, your God, who brought you out of the land of Egypt."[16]

Ex. 19:4 provides a brief survey of those marvelous deeds which preceded the Sinai experience. Through the recital and acknowledgment of such deeds the listener of each generation is brought to the foot of Sinai, as it were, to hear the "saving word." *Magnalia* of grace such as these are fundamental to the faith of Israel from the earliest times. They are the divine credentials, the vibrant acts of jealous interference, the *ṣidqōt Yahweh*, the content of God's activity in time, the antithesis to current mythology. In addition, however, they are the victories of a simultaneous conflict tradition that discerns more than the accidents of history in the events of the past. They are conquests which denude the so-called gods of the enemy.

(c) A Jealous Overlord. If it is true that the witness impact of Israel's personal historical experience in Egypt was unique and that the saving deeds of Yahweh are abnormal intrusions of God at given moments in time, then Theodorus Vriezen does well to emphasize that the covenant "relationship between Yahweh and Israel is not looked upon as natural but as placed in history by Yahweh."[17] It is Yahweh who offers the covenant, states the terms of the covenant, and establishes the covenant. And all of this is but the "giving" of grace, the option of the overlord. "If you hearken to my voice . . . and if you keep my covenant," (Exod. 19:5) is no cruel imposition. Allegiance is the natural response of those upon whom the witness has made its ultimate impact. "If" means quite reasonably "if you are willing." And the decision of acceptance inevitably involves the subsequent blessing of jealous and persistent love for a personal people. Here there is none of the caprice of Anath and her ilk. The attendant stipulations present the relevant way of life in the kingdom of the suzerain.

Such is the specific covenant (*bẹrīt*), later ratified with blood at the holy mountain of Sinai (Exod. 24:5-11).[18] If the forthright *'attā* (Exod. 19:5) emphasizes the urgency of the decision at that hour, then *'im* plus the infinitive absolute heightens the seriousness and absolute nature of Israel's allegiance.[19] Israel must respond to a "jealous" overlord and realize that all other gods stand in opposition to Yahweh. The conflict continues on several fronts, and the oath of allegiance reflects the total commitment of this people to a jealous God, "All that Yahweh has said we will do" (Exod. 19:8; 24:7). Under these conditions Yahweh reigns supreme; He alone can be King in Israel.

(d) A Sovereign Choice. Perhaps the most arresting statement of the present pericope is that which provides the very basis for the sovereign claim of Yahweh over Israel. The assertion that "all the earth is mine" (Exod. 19:5b) has as its inevitable corollary "all the peoples of the earth, and their gods, are under my control." Since such a statement implies a universal supremacy, many have sought to explain it as an editorial reflection of a later age.[20] Nevertheless, in addition to the fact that heroic gods of the ancient Near East made somewhat similar claims,[21] the preceding "conflict" tradition makes this divine assertion totally relevant and legitimate. Yahweh has just defeated the mightiest powers of nature and men.[22]

If Yahweh can give Egypt as a ransom for Israel, then His authority and domain are unlimited (cf. Isa. 43:1-7) and His choice is a sovereign election. This inevitably means that "the chosen one" is holy, that is, peculiar and unique by virtue of that choice (Exod. 19:6), selected as "the one" from among many. Furthermore, while it is in a sense correct to say that "Yahweh God of Israel and Israel people of Yahweh is a cliche without real content which *mutatis mutandis* could be used for other folk religions,"[23] the distinguishing features of Israel's choice as the *'am Yahweh* are the divine initiative exhibited in the historical moment of conflict and the specific covenant structure within which this election is exercised. Yahweh "became" bound, or rather He bound Himself to Israel, and the form of that bond was a covenant treaty. Israel's neighbors were bound to their gods by the forces of myth. Their history had not been disrupted by a distinctive covenant decision, for their conflict tradition was but the perennial cycle of creation and fertilization.

The technical terms *segullā, mamleket kōhạnīm*, and *gōi gādōš* express the "holy" aspect of Israel as a chosen people. *Sẹgullā* emphasizes the patient and cherished selection of divine love;[24] *mamleket kōhạnīm* delineates Israel's role as that of priest and mediator among various earthly nations; while *gōi qādōš* stresses the "other," separate character of Israel within its cultural environment.[25] As such, the nation Israel was born from the womb of conflict and endowed with this peculiar character in order that it might survive the imminent crises and temptations of youth.

In brief then, the essential features of the Sinai covenant which are brought into clearer focus through an awareness of the framework of a conflict tradition are the inculcation of Israel's acute sense of personal involvement in a particular historical act of revelation, its insistence upon the divine *magnalia* as redemptive victories against formidable foes and cosmic forces, its portrayal of the free option of a covenant obligation at the hand of a supremely jealous suzerain lord of history, and the emphasis on its own abnormal choice and its role as the privileged people of an almighty sovereign. These elements must be kept in mind in the following treatment of the history of the covenant amid conflict during the early days of Israel, and in the subsequent analysis of the archaic poetic materials of Israel. This nucleus will provide the necessary basis of comparison and point of departure for an investigation of the impact of Canaanite religions upon the faith of the Israelite. The first test of that covenant faith came at Sinai itself.

The Covenant Renewal at Sinai

The golden calf incident is the expression of an internal religious crisis, the outburst of rebellious tribes. Is it possible, however, to consider the golden calf crisis in any sense a part of the Sinai history and, therefore, a legitimate part of the ancient conflict tradition. Is not the very *raison d'être* of this incident the aberrations of Jeroboam I in I Kings 12:28?[26] In the opinion of the writer there are at least two factors which argue for the probable historicity of the essential features of the tradition. First, it seems highly unlikely that Jeroboam could have gained ready support for the introduction of bull images in connection with the worship of Yahweh, especially within the official priesthood, if there had been no such precedent from the sacred past.[27] Second, the representation of the hero of the Aaronide priesthood in such a disgraceful light does not reflect any later well-documented historical development.[28]

Moreover, the plausibility of the bull image being in vogue in the Mosaic age cannot be ignored.[29] In point of fact there are several indications that this conflict tradition reflects a major clash of Israelite tribes with the widespread culture of Canaanite mythology in which the bull motif is quite common.[30] A name such as Baal-Zephon immediately suggests the worship of the Canaanite Baal in this area.[31] In fact the crossing of the Reed Sea is located by the writer ". . . in front of Baal-Zephon" (Exod. 14:2ff.). Accordingly, Baal associations (and therefore the bull cultus) may well have impressed the Israelite tribes in Egypt and have been related to the exodus stream of tradition as the action of Jeroboam seems to imply.

The context makes it clear that the sin of Israel was nothing short of rebellion against the Sinai covenant, and therefore an offense to the Jealous One. This offense apparently involves more than making a pedestal for Yahweh comparable to the ark, although this may well have been true in the case of Jeroboam's calf.[32] Cherubim seem to have constituted the base of Yahweh's throne over the ark. The cherubim symbols prevalent in Palestine and Syria were apparently winged sphinxes.[33] If the dilemma of Aaron was the choice of a symbol for the divine throne, then the alternative could simply have been a winged sphinx or a winged bull (similar to those in Assyria). If this were the case, the choice of the latter would hardly have induced the harsh condemnation found in Exod. 32:30-33. What Israel actually experienced was the terrifying probability that Yahweh might Himself annul the covenant (32:10).

The fall of the house of Israel was serious on three counts. First, the demand of the impatient crowd to ". . . make us gods who will go before us," involves more than the rejection of Moses as its wilderness guide. The fabrication of gods immediately introduces a polytheistic attitude and with the degradation of Yahweh the mortal conflict is renewed. Although the cry of Jeroboam could be translated, "Behold your God, O Israel. . . ." (I Kings 12:28), the confession of Aaron in Exod. 32:4 is best rendered, "These are your gods, O Israel. . . ." Such an exclamation is nothing short of flouting the sovereign claim of Yahweh–the covenant Lord. This is true despite the fact that the attendant feast was supposedly in honor of Yahweh (Exod. 32:5). It is no longer Yahweh alone who is credited with the victory of the exodus redemption. And this is intolerable hypocrisy.

The second count against Israel was the bull image itself. As noted above, the presence of an image in a subordinate role as a throne base would hardly have evoked such fierce condemnation. If, on the other hand, this image is a representation of Yahweh Himself it would prove misleading, to say the least. The most obvious associations are with the Baal religions of Canaan. Whether Yahweh is humiliated by being forced into the attire of Baal, or whether this was an early equation of Yahweh with Baal, the implications are outrageous for the God of Israel. That the bull image was an idol, and therefore obnoxious, is supported by the divine comment, ". . . they have worshipped it and sacrificed to it" (Exod. 32:8), and by the subsequent reflection of Deut. 9:6-21.

In the third place it must be recognized that there is a pagan element connected with the worship ritual itself. Eating and drinking are the normal ways of expressing intimate communion with the divine, but the additional remark that ". . . they rose up to play" appears to be significant (Exod. 32:6). It would seem highly probable, then, that Canaanite fertility rites of some kind were associated with the feast.[34] The comment of Exod. 32:19 states that the anger of Moses was aroused by both the calf and the dancing. In other words, pagan polytheism, pagan idol imagery, and pagan cultic practices are probably depicted in this portrait of defection. The conflict between the worship of Yahweh and the fertility religions had taken on new dimensions.

This particular conflict tradition underscores certain additional features of the early faith of Israel. From the outset any visible representation of Yahweh was taboo (cf. Exod. 20:4). The face of Yahweh is not that of a calf but that of a forbidden glory (Exod. 33:17-23). To represent that terrible "unseen" with the forms of pagan culture meant breaking the covenant between Israel and Yahweh. The only recourse was to the sovereign grace which first tendered the covenant option. Only then could the covenant be renewed.

Further, the influence of rival cultic aberrations reached the very priesthood itself. Aaron stood condemned and the fate of Israel as the *'am Yahweh* was left hanging in the balance of divine jealousy and love. The radical nature of the conflict helps to underscore the unlimited mercy of the suzerain who can "repent of the evil" his jealous wrath demands. Forgiveness of sins is possible with the God of Israel (Exod. 32:7-14). All of this is totally consonant with the portrait of early Yahwism outlined above (cf. Exod. 34:6f).

The broken and duplicate tables of stone apparently symbolize the broken and renewed covenants respectively. The tables of testimony (*'ēdūt*) (Exod. 31:18) are the tables of the covenant.

In spite of proposed literary analyses of Exod. 34:1-28, however, these tables of stone pose a problem of interpretation.[35] Both Exod. 34:1-4 and 34:28 seem to refer back to the original ten *dẹbārīm* formulated on the first tables. Why, then, is the so-called "ritual decalogue" (Exod. 34:11-26) introduced at this point and made part of the covenant renewal situation?

If one takes seriously the preceding conflict tradition of the golden calf as outlined above, there seem to be two plausible answers to this problem. It is immediately apparent that this legislation is concerned with the crisis of life for the Israelite in Canaan. Hence, it is precisely the Canaanite religious culture, of which the Israelites toasting the golden bull had received a foretaste, that these stipulations label as poison. All Canaanite cultic symbols are to be shattered, all Canaanite sacrifices are to be boycotted, all Canaanite women are to be spurned[36] while Canaanite agricultural festivals are to be modified to conform to the cultus of Israel.[37] There are certain simple Canaanite customs that are inexpedient for weak Israelites (Exod. 34:26).[38] Accordingly, the insertion of these religio-cultic demands at this point is both logical and topical.

A second suggestion would point to the cultic or liturgical connection with the context. Apart from certain technical cultic terminology of the text, the very juxtaposition of the festivals with the renewal of the covenant at Sinai would suggest that the festivals and cultic acts of Israel are the provided means of communion whereby the Israelite tribes in Canaan can regularly maintain and renew the covenant with Yahweh. Theoretically then, all festivals could be considered covenant renewal festivals.[39] This does not mean that the various covenant renewal incidents of Israelite history are but later historicizations of a cultic ceremony. On the contrary, it is precisely these historical conflicts which help to explain the nature of the covenant and the covenant faith of early Israel, and in this present instance the event is used to illustrate the theological connection between the covenant and the cultic festivals. It might be argued that by binding each of the festivals to the covenant, Israel was given the direction and the impulse to "de-Canaanize" these festivals, just as the removal of "Canaanite" images (Exod. 34:17)[40] was a regular feature of major historic covenant renewals in later times.[41] Exod. 34, then, is a relevant example for an appreciation of the conflict of Israel with its Canaanite environment.

If the relevance of this "ritual decalogue" is granted, then the significance of the covenant renewal at Horeb can be emphasized further. Its unity with that of Exod. 19:3-6 is striking. The witness impact is prophetic, however, and the mighty acts are described as the "marvels" of tomorrow (Exod. 34:10). These terrible acts of grace will provide the impetus for renewal of faith and covenant when the Israelites are living among the Canaanites (34:10). Moreover, the stipulations of the jealous overlord, "whose name is Jealous" (Exod. 34:14)[42] outline a relevant and living worship pattern that will strengthen the bond of covenant communion. By virtue of this precise legislation, Yahweh is advancing His sovereign claim of Lordship over the agricultural and pastoral society of Canaan. Total separation and total purification, then, remain the jealous obligation for the new life and land.

The Incident at Beth-Peor

Beth-Peor is the scene of another "battle of faith" that must be revisited. It is noteworthy, to say the least, how little attention scholars have paid to the relevance of this encounter for the faith and history of Israel. Nor has the probable association of this event with a covenant of Israelite tribes on the Plains of Moab been adequately investigated.[43] The present analysis of that conflict at Beth-Peor is designed to remedy at least one phase of that weakness.

Israel's harlotry at Shittim or Beth-Peor was no mere pecadillo. "Israel yoked himself to Baal of Peor" reports the biblical tradition (Num. 25:3). That the term "yoked" (*yiṣṣāmēd*) represents a euphemism for cult prostitution cannot be demonstrated absolutely. Nevertheless, the context points the finger of guilt at the daughters of Moab and characterizes the subsequent corruption as religious harlotry (*znh*),[44] while the ensuing reference to a loose Midianite maiden (Num. 25:6-9) suggests a similar association.

The seriousness of this atrocity was long remembered by those prophets whose oracles recalled Israel to the covenant of yore. Hosea claims that Israel's persistent attachment to Baal only adds to the disgrace of Shittim (Hos. 5:2; cf. Num. 25:1), for on that black day of Israel's youth the excitement of Yahweh's discovery of Israel as "grapes in the wilderness" turned to sour disgust. "Israel consecrated themselves to Baal" (Hos. 9:10)! They even "ate sacrifices offered to the dead" on that occasion, replies the psalmist (Ps. 106:28). Such a revolting apostasy can hardly be regarded as insignificant.[45]

Who then was Baal of Peor? There is no undisputed answer to this query. Hosea links this Baal with the Canaanite Baal of his own time. While it is true that *ba'al* can be applied as a general term meaning "lord," in those instances where the name Baal stands alone it seems probable that the Canaanite Baal, the "lord" *par excellence* of this region, is usually meant. Moreover, the Balaam oracles which precede the Beth-Peor account, are located on the high places of Baal (Num. 22:41).[46] Many scholars classify the god of Peor as one of the so-called local agricultural baals. It can be argued, however, that there were many manifestations of the one Baal rather than many Baals.[47] In any case, the fertility rites alluded to above are consistent with a Baal cultus, while the Psalmist's (106:28) allusion to sacrifices to the dead may well refer to sacrifices for Baal in the underworld.[48] The sin of Peor persists even in Canaan, presumably because a conflict with the same Baal prevails there (Josh. 22:17).

How, then, is this notorious downfall related to the covenant motif? Deuteronomy offers an answer which has, in the main, passed unnoticed. The overall covenant structure and covenant theology of Deuteronomy, as well as its ultimate purpose of effecting a covenant renewal, is widely recognized.[49] The striking feature which must be emphasized, however, is that side by side with the recurrent mention of a momentous assembly under Moses on "the other side of the Jordan,"[50] there are several references which place this event opposite Beth-Peor (Deut. 3:29; 4:26). Furthermore, there is nothing inherently improbable in the claim that Israelite tribes concluded a covenant ceremony in Transjordan and that Beth-Peor provides the location for this event.[51] On the contrary, the fourth chapter of Deuteronomy tends to confirm this claim.

After the writer has summarized the saving deeds of Yahweh he specifies Beth-Peor as the location of the assembled league of Israelite tribes (Deut. 1-3). These glorious deeds are an extension of the *magnalia* of grace so basic to the covenant faith of Sinai already outlined. The initial *wẹ'attā* of Deut. 4:1 defines the urgency of the covenant renewal moment (as in Exod. 19:5 above). In the continuous conflict with the forces of Canaan the very existence of the Israelite tribes as a "holy" people is at stake (Deut. 4:1-2). The witness impact on Israel (as in Exod. 19:4) must be sharpened. Thus Israel is reminded, "Your eyes have seen what Yahweh did at Baal-Peor (Beth-Peor); for Yahweh your God destroyed from among you all the men who followed the Baal of Peor; but you who held fast to Yahweh your God are all alive this day"(Deut. 4:3f.).

The redemption experienced by the tribes at Baal Peor corresponds to the release experienced in the exodus events of Exod. 19:4. Through these events, including the covenant curse of the plague,[52] the participants were motivated to covenant renewal. The activities at Beth-Peor, then, offer a relevant "conflict" tradition which helps to elucidate the original covenant of Deuteronomy.

The later elaboration of this theme in Deut. 4, which forms a prelude to the repetition of the statutes of the decalogue (5:1-21), and the formal conclusion of the covenant, is intimately connected with the specific motifs and terminology of the Sinaitic covenant (in particular Exod. 19:3-6). Specific details of the Sinai covenant experience are recalled (Deut. 4:9-14). There is a consistent repudiation of all idolatrous forms on the grounds "that Yahweh your God is a devouring fire, a jealous God" (Deut. 4:15-24).[53] And again it is this jealous overlord whose sovereign choice of Israel as His precious possession and whose salvation of this people from the mighty Egypt are so unique that they presuppose the uniqueness of Yahweh (Deut. 4:20,32-39). With due solemnity the covenant witnesses of heaven and earth testify to the warning of this jealous King against any corruption comparable to the golden calf or the Beth-Peor incident (Deut. 4:25f.). In short, the events of Beth-Peor offer a notable example of the conflict motif of Yahweh versus the gods of the land.

The Crisis at Shechem

The research of Martin Noth has underscored certain aspects of the historical relevance of the traditions associated with the covenant ceremonies of the amphictyony at Shechem.[54] In addition, however, these traditions are significant for an appreciation of the religious crisis which was an integral part of that historical development. The amphictyonic deity of Shechem was specifically designated "Yahweh, God of Israel."[55] A religious conflict between this God and the gods of Israel's tribal heritage was inevitable.

Names such as Baal Berith, Baal Gad, Baal Meon, Baal Tamar, Anath, Beth Anath, Beth Dagon, and Beth Shemesh were scattered throughout the land.[56] The *ḥerem* of the ancient holy war in Israel was bound up with the jealousy of Yahweh and His aversion to any symbols or reminders of Canaanite cultus.[67] In his zeal for Yahweh, Joshua is said to have hamstrung the horses and burned the chariots which were so symbolic of Canaanite power (Josh. 11:6-9).

After the fervor of each of the holy wars was spent, the very prosaic business of survival by settlement demanded agricultural techniques, Canaanite techniques. With cultivation there came the lure of fertility rites, the unfortunate snare of the hungry peasant as well as the prosperous wine merchant. Time and again the writer of Judges recalls how the chosen people of Israel "served Baals and Ashtaroth" and forsook Yahweh.[58] The large number of Astarte plaques and figurines in Late Bronze Age deposits in Palestine indicates the frequency of Israelite contact with this way of life.[59] Here, then, was a battle royal, for in the adoption of Canaanite culture the kingship of Yahweh was at stake. Wherever Israel established a compromising *modus vivendi* with the Canaanites this conflict was destined to continue.

One particular tradition relating to the conflict as Shechem may bring the background to the covenant scene into clearer focus. The *heros eponymus* of that city is Shechem, son of Hamor (Gen. 34:2), and the inhabitants are designated "sons of Hamor" (Gen. 33:9) or the "men of Hamor" (Judg. 9:28), the name Hamor meaning ass. These latter expressions have evoked considerable comment. W. F. Albright considers them picturesque characterizations for "members of a confederacy."[60] This conclusion is suggested by the expression "to kill an ass," which is apparently synonymous with making a covenant or treaty among the Amorites of the Mari documents.[61] The conclusion is supported by the very name of the Shechemite deity "El-berith" (Judg. 9:46), that is, "God of the Covenant," an epithet which strengthens the probability of some Amorite or Canaanite tribal confederacy being associated with this shrine at Shechem.

The checkered history of Israel-Canaan relations at Shechem begins in Genesis (34:1-35:4). The rape of Dinah was the unfortunate incident which led to the first intimate association of Israelites and Shechemites, an association which was apparently a covenant relationship. The condition and seal of the covenant is that of circumcision (cf. Gen. 17:10); the subsequent communion one of free intermarriage and cultural interchange (Gen. 34:13-17). Alas, the despicable action of Simeon and Levi turned this covenant into a curse.[62] It is at this locality, with its covenant associations, that Joshua mediates the covenant ceremony of the twelve-tribe league, despite the fact that no conquest of Shechem is mentioned in Joshua.[63]

Two features of the Shechem tradition are prominent. First, Joshua chooses a place which has covenant associations, a place at which the worship of Baal Berith, alias El Berith, was known. This move may in itself be an overture to non-Israelite groups to covenant with Yahweh. Second, the presence of Canaanite Baal worshipers at this former Canaanite shrine reveals a living religious and cultural tension behind the assembly of Shechem. Furthermore, the *Gattung* of Joshua 24 is a covenantal formulation closely related to Exod. 19:3-8,[64] and conforms admirably to the structure of the Hittite suzerainty treaties.[65] It is within this structure that the religious and polemical motifs become apparent. It is "Yahweh, the God of Israel" (vss. 2, 23) who is claiming complete vassalage over the "mixed multitude" (Exod. 12:38) now assembled at Shechem. The witness experience of the exodus from Egypt becomes the common heritage of all tribes (v.7). The victories of the conquest of Amorite, Moabite, and Canaanite territory are also related as part of their personal involvement with Yahweh—the King who delivers from the enemies' hand "into your very own hand" (vss. 8, 10, 11). Here, again, we must observe that there is no "revelation" of the divinity by observation of cosmic phenomena, but by the conscious, personal, contemporary, life and death battles against pagans. Yahweh was, above all, the Terrible Warrior.

The credo of *magnalia*[66] (vss. 2-13) maintains a divine selectivity and bias of grace that is inexplicable according to any mythopoetic concept of God. For here is a power unhindered by natural boundaries, a "landless" God who gives "the land of Baal" as a trophy to His helpless warriors. Here, then, the Baal worshiper meets a new kind of God, a God of a people, a personal God, a God who "takes" an Abram (v.3), "gives" an Isaac (v. 3), "sends" a Moses (v. 5), "rescues" from the mighty Egypt (v. 6) *ad infinitum,* and all without human inducement.

After the proclamation of saving deeds follows the paranesis. The moment of decision demands an immediate resolution of the conflict (Josh. 24:14-18). The paranesis is introduced by the technical conjunction *'attā* (v. 14), and the inevitable choice by the subsequent *'im* (v. 15). The various powers which participate in the conflict are "the gods which your fathers served beyond the River and in Egypt" (vss. 2, 14f.), "the gods of the Amorites in whose land you dwell" (v. 15), and Yahweh Himself. The precise identification of any of the deities involved is a precarious venture. What pagan deities had been worshiped by the patriarchal families and were still worshiped in Canaan is uncertain. A manifestation of the "bull" god may have been recognized by segments of Israelites in Egypt and later depicted as the golden calf (cf. I Kings 12:28). The Amorite and Canaanite gods of the land would quite naturally include Baal and his consort. Baal of Peor in the land of "the two kings of the Amorites" (v. 12) had already become a part of Israelite heritage. Baal Berit, the local god of Shechem, could not be discounted, nor could the parade of deities which could conceivably be represented by the non-Israelite clans within "Israel" itself, clans such as the Kenites, Kenizzites, Jerahmeelites, and Gibeonites, for example.[67] One thing is clear; this was a conflict of sizable proportions and with serious implications.

According to our text Joshua claims that the amphictyony

could only exist as a divine autocracy under Yahweh. Hence the half-truth implied in the reaction of the people who cry, "Far be it from us to forsake Yahweh to serve other gods" (v. 16), must be countered with the full realization that they had to forsake and remove all other gods as well.[68] Failure to do so is tantamount to an unforgivable sin. Thus Joshua's answer is an unequivocal challenge: "You are not capable of allegiance (*'bd*) to Yahweh, for He is a holy (*qādōš*) God, a jealous (*qannō'*) God who does not forgive your rebellion (*peša'*) or sin" (v. 19).

This juxtaposition of Yahweh as *'ẹlōhīm qẹdōšīm* and as *'ēl qanno'* calls for further comment. The adjective *qādōš* is applied to any within the sacred seventy on Mount Ṣapon. The *qannō'* of Yahweh's holiness, however, demanded more than the exuberant shout of a festive pantheon. In this passage we behold Yahweh excluding the cultic and religious recognition of all contending deities, not through the sympathetic ritual of a mythical battle, but by a fiat proclamation in the *hic et nunc* of a historical moment in Shechem. To the Canaanite mind this must have been both ridiculous and presumptuous. The subsequent jealous attitude of this God would be dependent upon the moral impulses of the *gōi qādōš* He had selected through this covenant and not upon the rhythmic impulses of natural and cosmic laws. When considered in this concrete situation as a living issue of ancient history, the pristine revelation of Israel appears as a fervid monolatory and a forceful practical monotheism, for Yahweh is never *qādōš* or *qanno' in abstracto!*[69]

Finally, it can be seen how the jealous overlord of the Sinai covenant reinforces the serious imposition of His will by a witness ceremony (vss. 22, 27) and by relevant religious stipulations (v. 25), while the covenant response of the assembly repeats the claim of Mount Sinai, "And we will hearken to His voice" (v. 24). In this covenant Israel is blessed, for Yahweh is *qannō'* not only for His name's sake, but for the sake of His elect. Hence it becomes evident that an appreciation of the historical conflict behind the covenant ceremony at Shechem yields a deeper understanding of the theology of the amphictyony as a living faith relevant to its age and in tension with the culture of its age.

In brief, the ancient prose traditions relating to the covenant crises of Israelite tribes at Sinai, on the Plains of Moab, and within the confines of Canaan, reveal a recurrent conflict between the religious demands of Yahwism and the religious culture of the environment, as well as a constant struggle between Yahweh and the resurgent mythical deities of Israel's heritage and neighbors. Against the background of these conflicts the essential aspects of a covenant theology are discernible—a witness involvement, the *magnalia* of liberation experiences, the passionate jeolousy of Yahweh as the victorious overlord, and the sovereign selection of Israel as a covenant people.

NOTES

[1] The following discussion presupposes the essential historicity of the Sinai event and its immediate connection with the Exodus event, despite the fact that the ancient credos make no explicit reference to the former. See especially J. Bright, *A History of Israel* (Philadelphia: The Westminster Press, 1959), pp. 114-16. Furthermore, inasmuch as the entire faith and history of Israel as a twelve-tribe league is inexplicable without the covenant structure as its foundation, it is legitimate to regard the essential features of the covenant and traditions, many of which reflect an archaic and stereotype literary format, as reflections of the earliest faith of Israel.

[2] This does not exclude the motif of Yahweh's association with the North in later Israelite literature. See Ezek. 1:4; 28:14; Isa. 14:13; Ps. 48:3.

[3] See Exod. 7:3, 4; 11:9-10; 12:12. Compare Deut. 4:34; 28:46; *et passim.*

[4] It is inadequate to translate *psḥ* as "pass over" for it obscures the distinction between this word and *'br* which is also used in this section. *'br* is employed when the Destroyer passes over, but *psḥ* is used when Yahweh is present to save Israel. Further, in the light of the parallel with *nṣl* "to deliver, spare" in verse 27, and the parallel verbs in Isa. 31:5, it seems preferable to translate *psḥ* as "protect" or "stand guard." It is a term then which underscores the jealousy of Yahweh.

[5] See S. R. Driver, *The Book of Exodus* in *The Cambridge Bible for School and Colleges* (Cambridge: The University Press, 1953), pp. 57ff.; C. J. Rylaarsdam, *The Book of Exodus* in *The Interpreter's Bible* Nashville: Abingdon Press, 1952), pp. 894f. This conflict tradition is not confined to anyone particular literary strata of the Pentateuch.

[6] Note especially Exod. 15:24; 16:2,7,8,9,12; 17:3 for the "murmur" motif in Exodus. The same root (*lwn*) is found in Numbers (14:2,27,29,36; 16:11,41; 17:5) where murmuring implies breach of covenant. Compare also G. Mendenhall, *Law and Covenant in Israel and the Ancient Near East* (Pittsburgh: The Biblical Colloquium, 1955), p. 39.

[7] The archaic character of both the decalogue and the covenant code in general is widely recognized. No undisputed parallels to the biblical apo-

dictic law have yet been found. Note the suggestions of G. Mendenhall, "Ancient Oriental and Biblical Law," *Biblical Archeologist*, XVII (1954), 30; S. Gevirtz, "West Semitic Curses and the Problem of the Origins of Hebrew Law," *Vetus Testamentum*, XI (1961), 137-58.

[8] Exod. 10:22-26; 22:27-30; 23:1-19; 22:17,19,20,21.

[9] The apodictic laws are, of course, but part of the legislation which is appended to the Sinai covenant. Such a corpus of legislation, as G. Mendenhall has shown, is typical of archaic covenant structure and corresponds quite closely to the stipulations which form an integral part of the ancient Hittite treaties, in which no relationships with powers outside the Hittite Empire were permitted. The analysis of these restrictive laws as they pertain to the earliest history of Israel is not the immediate concern of this study. Suffice it to say that they serve to underscore the significance of the Sinaitic covenant as a historical treaty, a relic of the culture of its time, and a channel of divine communication. Mendenhall, *Law and Covenant*, pp. 31-41. For the connection of these laws with the covenant cultus of Israel see H. J. Kraus, *Gottesdienst in Israel* (München: Kaiser Verlag, 1954), pp. 43ff.

[10] Mowinckel classifies this passage as part of the ancient E stratum of tradition. S. Mowinckel, *Le Decalogue* (Paris: Felix Alcan, 1927), pp. 117, 128.; likewise G. Beer, *Exodus* in *Handbuch zum Alten Testament* (Tübingen: J. C. B. Mohr, 1939), pp. 96f.; and many others. The present writer agrees with the arguments of James Muilenburg, "The Form and Structure of Covenantal Formulations," *Vetus Testamentum*, IX (1959), 347-365f., that this passage is not to be considered a deuteronomistic addition as certain scholars have maintained. The literary and stylistic questions have been treated by Muilenburg, pp. 351-54.

[11] For the same technical expression in similar contexts see Exod. 20:22; Deut. 1:31; 29:1; Josh. 23:3.

[12] Compare the approach of G. Wright, *The Old Testament Against its Environment* (London: SCM Press, 1950), pp. 20-22.

[13] Deut. 3:21; 4:34; 7:19; 10:21; 11:2,7; 29:2; Josh. 24:7. Compare also Isa. 43:8-13 where Israel plays the role of Yahweh's star witness as the court of all the nations appears before Yahweh.

[14] It is apparent, however, that inanimate objects are employed as witnesses to certain covenants and oaths in the Old Testament, but never pagan gods. See Gen. 31:48-52; Deut. 4:26; Mic. 6:1; Josh. 22:34; 24:27. The above objects are not considered capable of reprisal in any way should one party break the oath. They appear more as memorial objects than as gods or powers comparable to the witnesses of pagan treaties. The pillars of Exod. 24:4 can well be understood in the same way. For Yahweh as witness see Judg. 9:7; Mic. 1:2; I Sam. 20:12,23,42; Zeph. 3:8.

[15] The role of Egypt as the classical enemy of Israel and consequently of Yahweh is apparent throughout the Old Testament. See for example Num. 3:13; Deut. 4:20; 6:21; 7:7,17-19; Judg; 6:8-10,13; Isa. 9:1ff.; Jer. 11:4; 46:1ff.; Ezek. 30:1ff.; Zech. 14:19; Ps. 81:6.

[16] Exod. 16:6; 18:1; 20:2; Lev. 11:45; 26:13,45; Deut. 6:12; Judg. 2:12; Ps. 81:11; *et passim*. A similar formula serves to underscore the saving activity of this God in the life of Abram. See Gen. 15:7.

[17] Th. C. Vriezen, *An Outline of Old Testament Theology* (Wageningen: Veenman & Zonen, 1958), p. 140.

[18] Studies on the suggested etymologies of *berīt* and the various nuances

of meaning associated with the term in its wider contextual usage are numerous. See for example, E. Jacob, *Theology of the Old Testament* (London: Hodder & Stoughton, 1958), pp. 209-17; J. Begrich, "Berit. Ein Beitrag zur Erfassung einer alttestamentlichen Denkform," *Zeitschrift für alttestamentliche Wissenschaft*, LX (1944), 1ff.; note also the extra-biblical form *TAR beriti* (cut a covenant) in the Qatna documents, W. F. Albright, "The Hebrew Expression for Making a Covenant in Pre-Israelite Documents," *Bulletin of the American Schools of Oriental Research*, CXXI (1951), 21-22.

[19] It is significant that both these literary expressions were preserved as technical marks of the covenant *Gattung*. For *'attā* in similar contexts see Gen. 31:44; Exod. 32:32; Deut. 4:1; 10:12; Josh. 24:14; 24:23; I Sam. 12:7, 13,14; *et passim*. *'im* plus infinitive absolute appears in typical contexts such as Exod. 15:26; 19:5; Deut. 8:19; 11:13f.; 11:22; 15:5; 28:1; Josh. 23:12f.; I Sam. 12:25; Jer. 7:5; 12:16; 22:4; Zech. 6:15. *'im* is, of course, a characteristic introductory particle in covenant contexts even where the infinitive absolute is not explicit. In this analysis the writer agrees with the findings of Muilenburg, "The Form and Structure of Covenantal Formulations," pp. 354-56.

[20] For example, H. Holzinger, *Exodus in Kurzer Hand-Commentar zum Alten Testament* (Tübingen: J. C. B. Mohr, 1900), pp. 64,67.

[21] Compare the title of Enlil, "Lord of heaven and earth," in *Hammurabi Code*, line 2; or Baal who is exalted as "Prince, Lord of the Earth," Baal V i 3f. These titles, of course, do not rule out the existence of lesser gods.

[22] The same theological perspective is apparent in the plague "battle" for example (Exod. 9:14,16,29), the exodus encounter (Exod. 14:4,18; 18:10f.) and the persistent motif of the humiliation of the mighty Egypt. Refer also to Exod. 34:10 and Josh. 3:11,13. For the development of this concept in Deuteronomy see Deut. 4:39; 7:6; 9:5; 26:19; *et passim.*

[23] Wright, *The Old Testament Against its Environment*, p. 15.

[24] For an appreciation of the concept of *sẹgullā* see Deut. 7:6-8; 14:2; 26:18f.; Ps. 135:4; Mal. 3:17. Note how it stands in parallel relation to *bāḥar* in Ps. 135:4. Compare also Mosche Greenberg, "Hebrew segulla: Akkadian sikiltu," *Journal of the American Oriental Society*, LXXI (1951), 172-74.

[25] The expression *gōi qādōš* militates against regarding this passage as a deuteronomic addition. The equivalent in Deuteronomy always appears as *'am qādōš*, e.g., 7:6; 14:2,21; 26:19; 28:9. A later editor would hardly have invented a *hapax legomenon* if he wished to achieve uniformity of tradition in an earlier manuscript. Compare also the position of Jacob, *Theology of the Old Testament* p. 204.

[26] This is virtually the position of M. Noth, "Das Zweite Buch Moses," *Das Alte Testament Deutsch* (Göttingen: Vandenhoeck & Ruprecht, 1959), p. 126. For an analysis of Noth's position see S. Lehmung, "Versuch zu Exod. 32," *Vetus Testamentum*, X (1960), 16-50.

[27] Further, to hail the bull image with the exclamation, "Behold your god (or gods) O Israel, which brought you out of the land of Egypt" would hardly be applicable and effective for Jeroboam's desired goals if the imagery was derived from some contemporary bull cult. By such an exclamation, it would seem, Jeroboam is linking his bull cultus form with a specific "exodus" tradition, thereby giving it an air of respectability and cogency. Moreover, if the Exodus story of the golden calf is a polemic against the action of the Northern Kingdom, one wonders why Israel as a whole stands condemned and not merely certain tribes from the North.

Note also W. F. Albright, *Archeology and the Religion of Israel* (Baltimore: Johns Hopkins Press, 1953), p. 219, n. 100, where he emphasizes that Jeroboam "posed as a reformer."

[28] The assumption that the polemic is against a false priesthood of Jeroboam which claimed to be the legitimate sons of Aaron goes beyond the evidence and ignores the fact that the story reflects upon the name of all descendants of Aaron, whether in Jerusalem or Bethel.

[29] W. F. Albright, *From Stone Age to Christianity* (New York: Doubleday & Co., 1957), pp. 298-301; Wright, *The Old Testament Against its Environment*, p. 25. The arguments against regarding the calf representation of Exod. 32 as being that of an Egyptian deity seem plausible, Driver, p. 348. Compare, however, the Rabbinic tradition in the hymn for the seventh day of Passover which says that the Israelites camped "before Baal-zephon, the last of their idols, spared as it were for their own undoing;" quoted from W. Heidel, *The Day of the Lord* (New York: The Century Co., 1929), p. 130, who investigates further possible associations between Baal-zephon and Egyptian deities, pp. 447-49.

[30] Both El and Baal are associated with bull imagery. Baal actually copulates with a heifer, Baal I v 18-22. For the illustration of Baal standing on a bull see G. E. Wright, *Biblical Archeology* (Philadelphia: The Westminster Press, 1957), p. 148. Baal is quite frequently represented as having horns. For the concept of El as a bull see M. Pope, *El in the Ugaritic Texts* (Leiden: E. J. Brill, 1955), pp. 35-42.

[31] For recent discussions of Baal-Zephon see W. F. Albright, "Baal-Zephon" in *Festschrift Bertholet* (Tübingen: J. C. B. Mohr, 1950), pp. 1-4, who cites a text to show the possibility of Baal-Zephon worship in Egypt also; O. Eissfeldt, "Baal Zephon, Zeus Casios, und der Durchzug der Israeliten durchs Rote Meer" in *Beitrage zur Religionsgeschichte des Altertums* (Halle: Max Niemeyer, 1932), I. That Baal-Zephon is to be identified with the Canaanite storm god Baal seems clear from the title of Baal in Keret II i 6f, which reads in the translation of Driver, "The valleys of Baal-Zephon weep for thee, father, the district of Kadesh does groan." Further, the home of Baal is in the North, Baal V iva 37f.; II iv. 18f.; *et passim*. See also A. S. Kapelrud, *Baal in the Ras Shamra Texts* (Copenhagen: G. E. C. Gad, 1952), p. 57.

[32] Albright, *From Stone Age to Christianity*, pp. 298-301; Wright, *Biblical Archeology*, pp. 147f.

[33] Note II Sam. 22:11; Ps. 18:11; I Kings 7:36; I Sam. 4:4. W. F. Albright, "What were the Cherubim?" *Biblical Archeologist*, I (1938), 1-3.

[34] J. C. Rylaarsdam, *The Book of Exodus*, p. 1064. Noth, "Das Zweite Buch Moses," p. 204, points to Gen. 26:8 as an illustration of the conjugal association of the Piel of *ṣḥq*.

[35] Many scholars assign the major portions of Exod. 34:1-28 to the J stratum. See S. R. Driver, *The Book of Exodus* pp. xxviii, 363-65; Noth, "Das Zweite Buch Moses," p. 214.

[36] Exod. 34:11-13,15-16. These verses are quite generally regarded as a deuteronomistic edition. The above observations, however, are still in order. The danger of Israelites forming a covenant with Canaanites existed from the very beginning (cf. Josh. 9). Furthermore, this situation can only be relevant to the period when the *inhabitants* of Canaan were a force in the land. In later periods it was possible for Israel to make covenant with Canaanite gods, but not Canaanite inhabitants.

[37] The Feast of Weeks, the Feast of Ingathering, and the offering of first

fruits of the ground are clearly agricultural in nature. They correspond closely to those included in the covenant code (Exod. 23:14-19. See E. Auerbach, "Die Feste im alten Israel," *Vetus Testamentum*, VIII (1958), 1-18; N. Snaith, *The Jewish New Year Festival* (London: SPCK, 1947), pp. 23ff.; J. Pedersen, *Israel* (London: Oxford University Press, 1940), III-IV, 415ff.

[38] The injunction not to boil a calf in its mother's milk is now to be linked with the Canaanite religious practice illustrated in the agricultural fertility ritual texts of Shachar and Shalim 1:13f. Cf. Exod. 23:19; Deut. 14:21. Note also A. de Guglielmo, "Sacrifice in the Ugaritic Texts," *Catholic Biblical Quarterly*, XVII (1955), 77f. The ritual element of this practice is emphasized by T. Gaster, "A Canaanite Ritual Drama," *Journal of the American Oriental Society*, LXVI (1946), 61f.

[39] In practice it seems that the Festival of Sukkoth was most frequently associated with covenant renewal, Deut. 31:9-11; I Kings 8:2ff.; Neh. 8:13ff. The passover seems to be connected with covenant renewal in IIKi. 23. The covenant renewal in I Sam. 12 occurs on the day of "wheat harvest" which would logically correspond to the Feast of Weeks. For the covenant renewal festival question see Kraus *Gottesdienst in Israel*, pp. 49ff. Cf. A. Weiser, "Die Psalmen," *Das Alte Testament Deutsch* (Gottingen: Vandenhoeck und Ruprecht, 1959), 14ff. On I Kings 23 see G. Widengren, "King and Covenant," *Journal of Semitic Studies*, II (1957), 2ff.

[40] It is interesting to note that the image forbidden in Exod. 34:17 is a *massēkā*, the very term used of the golden calf (32:4) while the parallel stipulation in Exod. 20:4 forbids the use of a *pesel*.

[41] II Chron. 29:10ff.; 31:1-3; 34:31-33; cf. 14:1-5.

[42] The expression "His name is Jealous" in 34:14 argues for the authenticity of this verse as part of the "ritual decalogue," since it is a *hapax legomenon* and totally consistent with the earliest covenant characteristics of Yahweh. Cf. Exod. 20:5; Deut. 4:24; Josh. 24:19.

[43] Lehmung, "Versuch zu Exod. 32," pp. 28-31, for example, suggests that Num. 25:1-5 and the kernel of the Golden Calf narrative arise out of the same historical milieu within the Israelite amphictyony. Its significance for Deuteronomy is ignored.

[44] That the "harlotry" of Israel was associated with cult prostitution seems evident from Hosea. See for example 1:2; 2:1-13; 4:11-14; *et passim*. Note also Deut. 23:17f.

[45] Cf. Mic. 6:5; Joel 3:18; Deut. 4:3.

[46] It is possible that the Baal-meon built by Mesha in Moab was dedicated to the Moabite God Chemosh, rather than to Baal, but not necessarily so. The Moabite stone describes a later *ḥerem* incident which refers to the Moabite God as Ashtar-Chemosh. This name, in itself, may imply a Moabite-Canaanite syncretism.

[47] We would suggest further that *bẹʿālīm* may be a so-called plural of majesty similar to Ashtaroth (Deut. 1:4, etc.) and Elohim. See G. E. Wright, "The Temple in Syria Palestine," *Biblical Archeologist*, VII (1944), 69f. Peculiar characteristics of Baal may have been emphasized by the needs of a local cultus, but ultimately it was the same Baal. Recall the numerous titles for Baal in the Ugaritic texts! Baal-Zebul, Baal-Kanap, Baal-Ṣapon and Aliyan-Baal are not distinctive deities but names which emphasize a particular aspect of Baal as he is "revealed" in Canaanite mythology.

48 Ps. 106:28. For sacrifice at the burial of Baal see Baal I i 15ff.

49 See Deut. 5:2f.,22-33; 11:26; 26:16-19; 27:9f.; 29:1; 30:15-20.

50 Num. 33:50ff.; 26:1-4; Deut. 1:1,5; 9:1; 31:1 *et passim.*

51 The significance of this covenant ceremony for the problem of the conquest of Canaan cannot be presented here.

52 That the plague represents a conscious polemic against another Canaanite deity is not demonstrable. It is of interest, however, that Reshep, an infrequent companion of Baal, is a god of pestilence. Cf. Hab. 3:5 and W. F. Albright, "The Psalm of Habakkuk," *Studies in Old Testament Prophecy* (Edinburgh: T. & T. Clark, 1950), p. 14.

53 That astral worship was prevalent within the Canaanite religion itself from the earliest times seems highly probable in the light of recent studies. Accordingly, to make Deut. 4:19 a criterion for dating this chapter is out of place. See J. Gray, *The Legacy of Canaan* (Leiden: E. J. Brill, 1957), pp. 123ff.

54 Noth, "Das Zweite Buch Moses," pp. 91-97. Compare Bright, *A History of Israel,* pp. 143-47.

55 Josh. 8:30; 24:2,23. Compare Gen. 33:20.

56 Judg. 8:33; Josh. 11:17; 12:7; Num. 32:38; Judg. 20:33; 3:31; Josh. 19:38; 19:27; 15:10; 13:17 *et passim.* For a discussion of the frequent use of Baal in later Israelite names such as Jerubbaal (Gideon) see Kapelrud, *Baal in the Ras Shamra texts,* pp. 43f.

57 Deut. 20:10-18; 7:17-26; Josh. 8:24-28; 11:12,20. The studies of G. von Rad, *Studies in Deuteronomy* (London: SCM Press, 1953) pp. 45-59, on the archaic character of the holy war passages in Deuteronomy are relevant at this point.

58 Judg. 2:11,13; 3:7; 6:28-32; 8:33; 10:6,10. Cf. also M. Noth, *The History of Israel,* (London: A. and C. Black, 1958), pp. 141-53.

59 Albright, *Archeology and the Religion of Israel,* p. 114.

60 *Ibid.,* p. 113. The main difficulty with this theory is the absence of any reference to killing the animal in question. An ancestor could be called an ass for various reasons. Cf. Gen. 49:14.

61 J. Pritchard, *Ancient Near Eastern Texts Relating to the Old Testament* (Princeton: Princeton University Press, 1955), p. 482.

62 The writer prefers the arguments of H. H. Rowley in favor of placing this incident prior to the descent into Egypt, rather than to consider it a reflection of the first efforts of conquest after the return from Egypt, as Noth has done. See H. H. Rowley, *From Joseph to Joshua* (London: Oxford University Press, 1950), pp. 111-29, and Noth, *The History of Israel,* pp. 70f.

63 It was to Shechem that Rehoboam went for his coronation, despite the fact that the ark and temple were in Jerusalem (I Kings 12:1).

64 Cf. Muilenburg, "The Form and Structure of Covenantal Formulation," pp. 357-60. Even if one holds the position of Noth, *History of Israel,* p. 92, that this passage has received its present format by virtue of regular repetition of the ceremony described therein, the subsequent conclusions concerning the basic theology of the amphictyonic covenant need not be radically affected thereby.

65 See the selection of Pritchard, *Ancient Near East Texts* pp. 201-06.

66 The significance of the ancient credos in Josh. 24:2-13, Deut. 6:20-25, and 26:5-10 is studied by G. von Rad, "Das formgeschichtliche Problem des

Hexateuch," *Gesammelte Studien* (München: Kaiser Verlag, 1958), VIII, 11-20.

[67] The presence of non-Israelite groups within Israelite society and even within the covenant league is apparent in passages such as Exod. 12:38; Num. 12:1; Lev. 24:10; Josh. 9:14; Num. 10:29-32; Judg. 1:16; Josh. 14:14f.; I Sam. 27:10; and suggested by the very chapter under discussion.

[68] The process of purging false gods at Shechem immediately reminds one of Gen. 35:1-4, where it is told that Jacob buried all the foreign gods under the sacred oak at Shechem.

[69] It can be argued with some cogency that the basic portrait of Yahweh as a jealous God presented in Joshua 24 reflects a pre-deuteronomic tradition. Apart from the general affinities to the E stratum tradition, the very term *qannō'* is not likely to be a deuteronomic redaction inasmuch as the form used in Deuteronomy is always *qannā'*.

Chapter II

THE FAITH OF ISRAEL IN THE EARLY POETIC TRADITIONS

THE POETIC EXPRESSION OF A PEOPLE'S CONVICTIONS IS often just as vital and poignant as that of its creedal counterpart. The archaic poetry of Israel is a particular case in point. The purpose of the present chapter is to present a preliminary summary of the basic religious convictions of Israel to be found in that corpus of poetic materials which is generally considered archaic.[1] The substantial unity of the fundamental religious beliefs delineated in the conflict traditions of the previous chapter and the essentials of faith presented in the archaic poetry should be readily apparent. A consideration of the poetic materials at this point, it is hoped, will answer the charge that by some standards the premonarchic conflict traditions outlined above present an anachronistic portrait of early Israelite beliefs. The present summary[2] of the early poetic and hymnic affirmations of Israel's faith will also provide a relevant background and point of departure for the subsequent chapters in which is given a more detailed analysis of specific aspects of Israel's early faith in relation to its Canaanite environment as this is reflected in the Ugaritic materials.

The relevant corpus of texts which forms the basis of the following analysis includes Gen. 49:2-17; Exod. 15:1-18; Deut. 33:2-29; Jud. 5:2-31; Ps. 29:1-11; and the Balaam oracles.[3] Materials which are often assigned to a somewhat later period, but which incorporate much of the same imagery and grammatical usage, are Deut. 32:2-43;[4] II Sam. 22:2-51; Hab. 3:2-19[5]; and Ps. 68:1-35.[6]

The Warrior King and His Mighty Feats

The archaic poetry of Israel is a significant cultic and lyric witness to the earliest tribal experience of Yahweh as the warrior God who was consistently victorious against pagan gods and arms. These poems are a living testimony to the persistent conflict between Yahweh and the alien forces which threatened the existence of His people—Israel. The assembled tribes were called upon to recite the triumphs of their King, for through these *magnalia* of victory the character of their God was revealed and the nature of His heavenly opponents exposed. "The greatness of His majesty" was seen when he overthrew Israel's adversaries and shattered the enemy or when the violent blast of his nostrils checked the menacing deep (Exod. 15:6-8). Over Egypt He triumphed gloriously (Exod. 15:1); against the mighty foes of Israel he marched forth in theophanic splendor (Jud. 5:4f). Neither pagan gods nor deified cosmic forces could stay his onslaught. His victories displayed his incomparability (Exod. 15:11). For the prophet Balaam the survival of Israel was proof positive of Yahweh's efficacy and the helplessness of his own gods. No divination or enchantment could hinder the people of Yahweh (Num. 23:21-23). His right arm was "glorious in power" (Exod. 15:6). The so-called gods of pagan peoples were but heavenly weapons at His disposal (Jud. 5:20) or cosmic forces at His command (Jud. 5:21; Exod. 15:10). His voice, not the thunder of Baal, caused the earth to writhe (Ps. 29); His thunderbolts, not Reshep, brought the pestilence (Deut. 32:23f); His heavenly armies were at His side (Deut. 33:2), and His glittering sword exacted vengeance (Deut. 32:41). He overwhelmed the enemy with terror and dread (Exod. 15:16), petrified His foes, and stood erect with His foot on their backs (Deut. 33:29).[7] Even the earth shuddered at the advent of the King of Israel (Jud. 5:5). As the warrior King He led the conquering host of Israel to safety (Ex. 15:13) and preserved them from the dangers of the desert (Deut. 32:10-12). He rode forth from the heavens to fight for Israel; He was both the sword and the shield of His people (Deut. 33:26,29). The enemies of Israel were inevitably the foes of Yahweh (Jud. 5:31).

These mighty feats of Yahweh, the "man of war," are a major thrust of the ancient poems. His *magnalia* of victory are glorious deeds worthy of epic recital; they are the *ṣidqōt Yahweh*, victorious acts of deliverance which reveal the character of the God of Israel. These divine acts of interference motivate Yahweh's exaltation as King and covenant overlord in Israel.[8] He has won the conflict. His deeds are exhaustive (*tāmīm*), reliable (*'ẹmūnā*), and consistently directed toward Israel's need (*mišpāṭ*). Therefore He is righteous (*saddīq*); He is the Rock of Israel (Deut. 32:4). His names,[9] too, reflect His character. He is Yahweh, man of war (Exod. 15:3), the incomparable Rock of Salvation,[10] the Mighty One of Jacob,[11] and King in Jeshurun (Deut. 33:5).

These poetic traditions provide a forceful testimony to the earliest consciousness of Israel concerning the decisive intervention of God. Through hymnic proclamation the Israelites tribes affirmed the character of their God as a deliverer whose advent was associated with historically identifiable incidents within their own tradition or experience. He was the personal warrior God who fought against the local foes of Israel and thereby humiliated the pretentious gods of the enemy or exposed the inefficacy of deified forces of nature. The jubilant affirmation, "Who is like thee, Yahweh, among the gods" is the necessary culmination of the conflict (Exod. 15:11).

The Sovereign Lord and His Chosen One

Yahweh, the Warrior of Israel, was also the sovereign Lord over all powers and beings. His mighty feats demonstrated His supreme authority. Because of these victorious deeds He was hailed as Yahweh, God of Israel. As might be expected the name Yahweh dominates the ancient poetic materials. In the Balaam oracles, however, the God of Israel is also identified as El, Elyon, and Shaddai.[12] According to the Ugaritic myths El was the overlord of the Canaanite pantheon. He is characterized as the creator of all creatures and the father of mankind.[13] The associations connected with this name, therefore, would imply a confession of Yahweh's role as the creator God who has final authority over all heavenly beings. Similar associations seem to be made with the names of Elyon and Eli.[14] The archaic cultic confession of Gen. 14:19 exalts the God, El Elyon, Creator of Heaven and Earth. It is plausible that Elyon may have been the creator god of the Phoenician pantheon and the grandfather of El.[15] In any case, the later assertion of the psalmist that "Thou alone, whose name is Yahweh, art Elyon over all the earth" (Ps. 83:19) seems to preserve the same ancient poetic tradition which confronts us here. A crucial passage in this connection is Deut. 32:7-14.

The correspondence between this passage and the basic text of Exod. 19:3-6 treated above is readily discernible. The sovereign claim that ". . . all the earth is mine" is paralleled by the assertion that the Most High God ". . . gave to the nations their inheritance . . . and fixed the bounds of the peoples" (Deut. 32:8). The *gōi qādōš* from among all peoples is here designated "Jacob His alotted heritage" while the precious *sẹgullā* is now cherished as the *'īšōn 'ēnō* "the pupil of His eye' (Deut. 32:9f.). The identical metaphor of a protecting eagle in the desert and the solitary guide in a hostile land are also apparent in both. The significant poetic parallelism of the key passage (Deut. 32:8f.) can be seen in the rendering:[16]

When the Most High distributed lots
    when he separated the children of man,
He set the borders of the peoples
    like the number of sons of God;[17]
But Yahweh's portion is His people,
    Jacob His allotted domain (heritage).

This parallelism and the context seem to demand that Elyon, the Lord of destinies, and Yahweh are one and the same person, regardless of the traditions which may lie behind these verses.

Over the total number of peoples[18] on earth the God of Israel exerts a sovereign claim; from among their number He makes a sovereign choice. The object of His choice is characterized as *ḥebel naḥalātō*, (Deut. 32:9). Such a term in its immediate context points to this one people as His own peculiar possession by virtue of a prior conscious selection, and not by virtue of some *a posteriori* incident or accident of history. Here the divine selection precedes the "historical" election. Yahweh is the Sovereign Lord as well as the Warrior of history. The designation of Israel as the *naḥalā* (inheritance) accentuates the personal, cherished, character of Israel as His *'am* or His "family property," rather than the concept of some nation handed down at the demise or injunction of a higher god.[19]

The "historical election" on the other hand is described with a wide variety of metaphors and imagery.[20] From the vantage point of Israel's personal experience it was like the sudden discovery of a foundling in the wilderness (Deut. 32:10) or the birth of an infant son (Deut. 32:6,18). The time and the date could be specified. For it was the day of redemption (Exod. 15:13),[21] the day of the exodus (Num. 23:21-23), the day of enthronement, and the day of the covenant (Deut. 33:2-5).

A sovereign choice and historical selection of this caliber inevitably involves a change on the part of the chosen. Israel is surrounded by the isolation of divine intervention. Israel is different by virtue of this interference; it is *qādōš* by virtue of this divine choice. And throughout this poetic corpus one can discern this awareness of being different, isolated, *qādōš*, because of Yahweh's self revelation in the election. The pagan prophet Balaam also senses this characteristic when he exclaims:

> How can I curse whom God has not cursed?
> How can I denounce whom Yahweh has not denounced?
> From the top of the mountains I see him;
> From the hills I behold him;
> Lo, a people dwelling alone (*lẹbādād*)
> Not counting itself among the nations. (Num. 23:8f.)

This *lẹbād* character of Israel is also apparent by virtue of Israel's being an *'am nōša'*, a "people saved by Yahweh" (Deut. 33:29), a nation "redeemed" and "begotten" (Exod. 15:13,16), His "workmanship" (Num. 23:23) and His newborn child (Deut. 32:10-12).

The term *qānā* in Exod. 15:16 calls for further comment. One demonstrable meaning of the root is "to create" or "to procreate."[22] The association of this term with the election of Israel is likewise significant. The elective choice of Israel in Exod. 15:16 is first underscored by the designation "Thy people." Elsewhere this Israel is specifically the "people belonging to Yahweh," the chosen host with Yahweh at its head, the amphictyonic covenant people who march forth triumphantly (Jud. 5:11.13). The text of Exod. 15:16 parallels the expression "Thy people" with the designation "the people whom Thou hast created." The significance of this characterization lies in the use of the archaic relative *zū* (cf. Exod. 15:13; Jud. 5:5) and the introduction of the verb *qānā*. This term is an integral part of the ancient title "Elyon, Creator (*qōnē*) of Heaven and Earth," as it appears in Gen. 14:16. The meaning of the concept is further elucidated in Deut. 32:6 which reads, "Is not He (Yahweh) your father who created (*qnh*) you, who made you (*'sh*) and begat you (*kwn* in Polel)".[23] In the early poetic tradition, then, it seems apparent that the creative activity of Yahweh as the sovereign God, as El the Creator of creatures, is concentrated upon the people of Israel and that the verb in question is virtually synonymous with Yahweh's redemptive and elective activity in Israel. Similarly, the title of El as *'ab 'ādām* suggests the sovereign creativity of El over all mankind.[24] When the title *'ab* is applied to Yahweh, however, the Israelites' attention is focused upon the election of Israel, the people of God. Yahweh is *'ab* only to Israel; there is no universal fatherhood of God. Israel, then, is His created, begotten son, His only son. The initiative in the selection of Israel always stems from Yahweh.[25]

Thus, as in the covenant contexts discussed earlier, the ancient hymnic and poetic tradition of Israel is acutely aware of Israel's role as something *qādōš*, different, cherished, selected, and historically created by a sovereign overlord. It is in and through this role that Israel must recognize its election and exercise its obligations.

The Covenant God and His Jealous Love

As the victorious covenant God of Israel, Yahweh is jealous of His own "holiness" and that of His covenant people. The predominance of the covenant name Yahweh has already been noted.[26] The amphictyonic title "Yahweh, God of Israel" is hailed by the poet of the Song of Deborah (Jud. 5:5).[27] This God is the jealous and holy Lord of the covenant (Jos. 24:19). Additional covenant associations are underscored by the parallel epithet "Yahweh, the One of Sinai" (Jud. 5:5), whose advent was linked with the Israelite tribes from the South (Jud. 5:4), whose theophanic intrusion originated from Sinai (Deut. 33:2), and whose exalted name was hailed as King in the tribal assembly (Deut. 33:3-5).

The *qādōš* and elect character of the covenant people Israel inevitably evokes Yahweh's jealous protection. Protective duties were a normal commitment of the suzerain in ancient covenant treaties. Similarly Yahweh's guardian zeal is aroused by His lively covenant love (*ḥesed*) as He leads His ransomed flock through the treacherous highways of the heathen (Exod. 15:13). His unseen disarming *'ēmā* (terror), the paralyzing radiation of His jealousy renders the enemy powerless so that His chosen sons may pass by (Exod. 15:15f.).[28] Yahweh Himself is the impregnable shield of the peculiar "saved" amphictyonic people of God (Deut. 33:29) and the avenging warrior of His chosen ones (Deut. 32:35f.). His battle cry has a similar ring of jealousy: "Where are their gods, the rock in which they took refuge?" (Deut. 32:27). The ancient prophet Balaam appreciates the implication of this divine jealousy for the holiness of Israel: "Blessed is every one who blesses you and cursed is every one who curses you" (Num. 24:9). Yahweh can never be neutral as far as His covenant congregation is concerned. The divine pathos of Yahweh is stirred whenever His experiment of love stands in jeopardy. "Whenever new gods were chosen, then war was in the gates" (Jud. 5:8). The earliest conflict traditions are a living testimony to the jealousy of this God in Israel.

This divine agitation, however, is also designed to preserve an inner rapport between the covenant overlord and His chosen people. All of the covenant tribes must acknowledge their covenant obligations (Deut. 33:4). Any who fail to come to the defense of His covenant name are severely rebuked (Jud. 5:15-17, 23). The provocation of Yahweh's jealous wrath is not simply a fashionable change of idols, but the desertion of the One who created the covenant people, the derision of the Rock who rescued this nation for a purpose (Deut. 32:15), indifference to the Father who begat (*yld*) these tribes for covenant sonship (Deut. 32:18), and the spurning of Him who went through the birth-pangs of election (*ḥūl*) on Israel's behalf (Deut. 32:18). Here there is none of the selfish revenge or rage of pagan deities who are peeved at the success of some mortal hero. These poetic texts present a sensitive responsibility to the total claims of the jealous overlord. The moment the Israelite even experiments with a new god there is an ignition of the divine zeal that executes a relentless course of vindication (Deut. 32:15-38).

A necessary corollary of Yahweh's jealous claims is the exaltation of His glory and the progressive elimination of the efficacy of all rivals. Strange gods must be exposed as "no-gods" (Deut. 32:17,21). Heavenly companions and earthly subjects alike must hail the surpassing glory of His holy name (Ps. 29:1f.; Jud. 5:3). The *magnalia* incited by His jealousy reveal Yahweh as a God infinitely superior to any other power or name. The Song of Miriam reaches its climax with the affirmation:

> Who is like thee among the gods, O Yahweh?
> Who is like thee, terrible among the holy ones?
> Awesome in laudable deeds!
> Performer of great feats! (Exod 15:11).

Likewise the Blessing of Moses motivates the ancient covenant people Jeshurun to exclaim:

> There is none like God, O Jeshurun,
> Who rides through the heavens to your help,
> And in His majesty through the skies. (Deut. 33:26)[29]

Ultimately, then, the jealousy of Yahweh involves a defense of His holiness and an exaltation of His supremacy. The outcome of Yahweh's crucial conflict with all pagan powers must be constantly acknowledged.

The articles of faith embodied in the early poetic materials are forthright affirmations of Yahweh's self-revelation through the military feats witnessed by the Israelite tribes, profound responses to Israel's historical election as a holy people, and dynamic proclamations of that divine jealousy which curbed Israel's sons and crushed Israel's foes. These hymnic confessions proclaim the same character and claim of the covenant God, the same activity and attitude of the God of Israel, the same vision and victory of Yahweh for Israel that is fundamental to the conflict traditions of the previous chapter. Israel's God is jealous and continues His polemic against all rival forces as Israel's religion comes into direct contact with that of its neighbors; for His mighty deeds, His revelatory acts, His self-expenditure on behalf of Israel are without equal.

NOTES

[1] For a discussion of the characteristics of archaic poetry see the articles by F. M. Cross and D. N. Freedman, "The Song of Miriam," *Journal of Near Eastern Studies*, XIV (1955), 237-50, and "The Blessing of Moses," *Journal of Biblical Literature*, LXVII (1948), 191-210. Compare also W. I. Moran, "The Hebrew Language in its Northwest Semitic Background," *The Bible and the Ancient Near East*, ed. G. E. Wright (New York: Doubleday & Co., 1961), pp. 54-72. Note also D. N. Freedman, "Archaic Forms in Early Hebrew Poetry," *Zeitschrift für die alttestamentliche Wissenschaft*, LXXII (1960), 101-07.

[2] For a more complete consideration of the poetic materials see the writer's doctoral dissertation "Conflict of Religious Cultures," Concordia Seminary, St. Louis, 1962.

[3] B. Vawter, "The Canaanite Background of Genesis 49," *Catholic Biblical Quarterly*, XVII (1955), 1-18. Cross and Freedman, "The Song of Miriam." Cross and Freedman, "The Blessing of Moses." F. M. Cross, "Notes on a Canaanite Psalm in the Old Testament," *Bulletin of the American Schools of Oriental Research*, CXVII (1950), 19-21. W. F. Albright, "The Oracles of Balaam," *Journal of Biblical Literature*, LXIII (1944), 207-33.

[4] The basic conclusions of this chapter are valid even if the reader is not willing to acknowledge an early date for the references from Deut. 32:2-43. Recent investigations into the archaic nature of the Song of Moses has been undertaken by W. F. Albright, "Some Remarks on the Song of Moses in Deuteronomy xxxii," *Vetus Testamentum*, IX (1959), 339-46, and by O. Eissfeldt, "Das Lied Moses Deuteronomium 32:1-43 und das Lehrgedicht Asaphs Psalm 78 samt einer Analyse der Umgebung des Moses-Liedes," *Berichte über die Verhandlungen der Sächsischen Akademie der Wissenschaften zu Leipzig*, Band 104, Heft 5 (1958). See also G. E. Wright, "The Lawsuit of God: A Form-Critical Study of Deuteronomy 32" *Israel's Prophetic Heritage* (New York: Harpers, 1962), pp. 26-67.

[5] Albright, "The Psalm of Habakkuk," pp. 1-18.

[6] W. F. Albright, "A Catalogue of Early Hebrew Lyric Poems," *The Hebrew Union College Annual*, XXIII (1950-51), 1ff.

[7] The translation "backs" for *bāmōt* in Deut. 33:29 seems preferable in the light of Baal I i 5; II iv 14f *et passim*. The concept of the "terror" of Yahweh is a significant part of the holy war traditions elsewhere. See footnote below.

[8] Exod. 15:18; Num. 23:21; Deut. 33:5; Ps. 29:10.

[9] The close relationship between name (*šēm*) and character is also reflected in the Ugaritic expression *'ṯtr-šm-b'l* in Keret II vi 56. The proclamation of the name (Deut. 32:3 *et passim*) is tantamount to a definition of character. See Baal III* A 11, 18, 19 and Shachar and Shalim i 21-23.

[10] For the use of the term Rock (*ṣūr*) see Deut. 32:4, 15, 18, 30, 31. The military associations of *ṣūr* are underscored by the usage in 2 Sam. 22:2,3,32ff, 47-49. Compare the designation of Yahweh as *'eben* (stone) in Gen. 49:24. The implication is that Yahweh is the "mountain fortress" of Israel. The archaic meaning of *ṣūr* as mountain is apparent from the Ugaritic (*ǵūru*). Compare Num. 23:9.

[11] The Hebrew term *'ābīr* is parallel to the Ugaritic *'ibr* (bull or buffalo). Baal sires an *'ibr* to the heifer Anat (Baal IV iii 20,35; Hadad i 32, ii 53-54). It seems probable, however, that the metaphor in Gen. 49:24 points to the strength rather than the fecundity of Yahweh.

[12] Num. 23:8, 22; 24:4,16; Compare Gen. 49:25; 2 Sam. 22:14; Ps. 7:18; 91:1f.

[13] For further details concerning the various epithets and attributes of El see Pope, *El in the Ugaritic Texts*, pp. 25-54.

[14] There is no indication that Eli and Elyon are to be equated. Baal is characterized as *'ly* in Keret II iii 4-8 but he is not identical with Elyon who is absent from the Ugaritic texts published to date. Some of the biblical passages where the vocalization *'ali* (for *'al*) is suggested are Deut. 33:12; I Sam. 2:10; Ps. 57:3; Hos. 7:16; 10:5; 11:8; Isa. 59:18; 63:7 *et passim*. For a detailed discussion see M. Dahood, "The Divine Name Eli in the Psalms," *Theological Studies*, XIV (1953), 452-57. For its presence in Deut. 32:12, see Cross and Freedman, "The Blessing of Moses," p. 204. See also the comments of G. R. Driver, "Hebrew *'al* (High One) as a Divine Title," *Expository Times*, L (1938-39), 92f.

[15] For a complete discussion of this problem, the evidence of Philo of Byblos, the reading from Karatepe *'el qn 'rṣ*, and the Ugaritic texts see Pope, *El in the Ugaritic Texts*, pp. 55-58, and G. L. Della Vida, "El Elyon in Genesis 14:18-20," *Journal of Biblical Literature*, LXIII (1944), 1-9. Compare the suggested introduction of the term into Israel by Jacob, *Theology of the Old Testament*, pp. 45-47. O. Eissfeldt, "El and Yahweh," *Journal of Semitic Studies*, I (1956), 29, appears to equate El and Elyon.

[16] Albright, "Some Remarks on the Song of Moses," p. 343.

[17] The reading "sons of God" instead of sons of Israel is now accepted by the majority of scholars. The evidence of the Septuagint and the Dead Sea Scroll text is published by P. Skehan, "A Fragment of the Song of Moses from Qumran," *Bulletin of the American Schools of Oriental Research*, CXXXVI (1954), 12-15. A discussion of the nature of the "sons of God," the "holy ones," and the "heavenly council" is reserved for a later chapter.

[18] For seventy as the sacred number for the totality of gods and of men see Albright, "Some Remarks on the Song of Moses," p. 343 and S. R.

Driver, *Deuteronomy* in *The International Critical Commentary* (Edinburgh: T. & T. Clark, 1902), pp. 355f.

[19] Note the use of *naḥalā* in Ps 68:10; 33:12; 106:5; Deut. 4:20; 9:26, 29; and also Exod. 15:17.

[20] Although the technical term *baḥar* is absent, synonyms such as *qānā, yālad, māṣā' pā'āl* et *alii*, as well as the nouns denoting Israel as the elect demonstrate the depth and extent of the election motif in less stereotype terminology.

[21] K. Galling's classic treatment of the election traditions begins with the exodus event portrayed in Exod. 15 as basic for the election consciousness of Israel, a motif which he then traces throughout the Old Testament. See K. Galling, *Die Erwählungstraditionen Israels* (Giessen: A. Töpelman, 1928), pp. 5f.

[22] The present writer's conclusion that the root *qānā* may have a second meaning of "create" or "procreate" is supported by the Ugaritic and confirmed by the work of P. Humbert, "Qānā en Hebrue Biblique," *Festschrift Bertholet* (Tübingen: J. C. B. Mohr, 1950), pp. 259-66; so also Pope, *El in the Ugaritic Text,* p. 51. See Ugaritic passages Keret I ii 4; Aqhat I iv 58; Baal II i 20, iii 25, 29, 34; IV iii 5. For biblical usage see Gen. 4:1; Exod. 15:16; Ps. 139:13; Prov. 8:22.

[23] As Pope, *El in the Ugaritic Text,* pp. 50f., has demonstrated, the Polel of the root *kwn,* when applied to the deity, can mean create or procreate, as the parallelism in Deut. 32:6 already indicates. The parallel verbs found in Job 31:15; Isa 45:18; and Ps. 87:5f. substantiate this. Furthermore, in Baal IV iii 5f. *qny* is parallel to *kwn* (with reduplicated nun) in a context which refers to Anat the cow giving birth to a calf sired by Baal the bull. See further Pope, p. 51. Compare also Pss. 8:4; 24:2.

[24] Compare the broad perspective of the father concept as applied to Nanna, "O father begetter of gods and men . . . ," and "Father begetter who looks favorably on all living creatures." See Pritchard, *Ancient Near Eastern Texts,* pp. 385f. The title *'ab'ādām* appears in Keret I iii 32, 47, vi 12, 31 and seems to be synonymous with the common epithet *bny bnwt* (creator of creatures).

[25] Compare the election of Cyrus: "He [Marduk] scanned and looked [through] all the countries searching for a *righteous* ruler willing to lead him [i.e., in the annual procession]. [Then] he pronounced the name of Cyrus, King of Ashan, declared him to be [come] the ruler of all the world," Pritchard, p. 315.

[26] The debate concerning the origin of the name Yahweh will not be entered into here. In any case, the testimony of the present text in no way conflicts with Exod. 6:2f. R. Abba, "The Divine Name Yahweh," *Journal of Biblical Literature,* LXXX (1961), 321, in a recent survey of the subject concludes that "Yahweh appears to have been a name peculiar to Israel and to have been borrowed from Israel when it occurs in the proper names of other tribes."

[27] See Jos. 24:2,23; Gen. 33:20 *et passim.*

[28] Compare Exod. 23:27; Jos. 2:9; Deut. 32:25; and frequently in Job. This terror almost appears to be an extension of the divine personality and the major psychological weapon of divine warfare.

[29] The suggested emendation of Cross and Freedman, "The Blessing of Moses," p. 209, is plausible: "Who rides the heavens mightily, who rides the clouds gloriously," and does little violence to the present text.

Chapter III

THE KINGSHIP OF BAAL AND THE KINGSHIP OF YAHWEH

A COMPARISON OF RELIGIOUS AFFIRMATIONS IS A LEGITIMATE part of research into the conflict or accommodation of contemporary cultures. Comparisons, however, are often precarious adventures of scholarship, while religious analogies are easily overdrawn in the excitement of discovering apparent similarities. The present analysis of the kingship of Baal and the kingship of Yahweh, therefore, must guard against such pitfalls, if at all possible. No attempt is being made, at the outset, to specify any actual borrowing or direct accommodation of religious essentials. The first step is simply to outline the essentials of kingship from textual sequences involving Baal and Yahweh, respectively, and to show how one adds to a deeper understanding of the other by virtue of comparable activities, striking resemblances, possible conflicts, or marked contrasts. By the expression "kingship sequence" is meant that progression or pattern of activity whereby divine kingship is acknowledged. It is the bold outline of this kingship sequence to which the reader is directed in this chapter.

THE PURPOSE AND NATURE OF THE UGARITIC KINGSHIP TEXTS

The hero of the Canaanite pantheon at Ugarit is Aliyan Baal, a name which defines the character of the fertility god *par excellence*. But Baal is not the lord of nature by divine right but by divine power. Baal is Aliyan; he is, as the name implies, "the victorious one," "the valiant warrior," or "the conquering hero."[1] Thus, in the first cycle of texts Baal's character as the warrior king is established,[2] while in the second the subsequent exercise of his kingship is made effective.[3] The immediate purpose of these texts, then, is the affirmation of this kingship character.

The Baal texts in general present myth in the strict sense of the term, for they deal entirely with the interaction of the gods. That these activities have cosmic significance is immediately apparent, but precisely what *Sitz im Leben* such myths had within the culture and cultus of the Canaanites is hotly disputed.[4] Nothing in the texts themselves specifies the dramatic liturgy or cultic ceremonies which are to accompany the recital or portrayal of the myth. Nevertheless, the prominent role which the temple of Baal plays in this sequence makes it highly plausible that these texts played some part in the actual temple cultus. In any case, the religious import of the material is evident, and the character of Baal as the sovereign lord of the cosmos is a legitimate subject of investigation despite the fact that we do not know the precise details of how the Baal temple acknowledged or reenacted the establishment of the same.

Baal's Decisive Battle for Kingship

The initial fragments of the myth depict Yam, with his exalted throne name of Yaw,[5] as a cosmic king who is inordinately jealous of his royal status. He gives vent to this jealousy by demanding the surrender of Baal, son of Dagan, from the hands of the pantheon:[6]

tn 'ilm d tqh	Give up, O gods, him whom you guard,[7]
d tqyn hmlt	Him, O host,[8] whom you protect,
tn b'l [w'nnh]	Give up Baal and his servants,
bn dgn 'artm pdh	The son of Dagan, that I may inherit his gold.[9]

When Baal first appears at the scene of the heavenly council he is cast as the champion of the humiliated, who himself must rise from servitude. But despite the heroic effort of Baal to arouse the convocation which stands terrified before the emissaries of Yam, El as titular head of the pantheon capitulates to Yam's demands with the reply:[10]

ʿbdk bʿl y ymm	Baal is your slave, O Yam!
ʿbdk bʿl [ṯpṭ nhrm]	Baal is your slave, Judge River!
bn dgn ʾasrkm	The son of Dagan your prisoner.

All of this serves to exaggerate the mammoth task of Baal and the glory of his subsequent conquest. He rises from slavery to kingship. All the odds and the gods are apparently against him. But more important, Yam now plays the role of the giant; he is the great and formidable opponent of Baal, as immovable as the sea whose name he bears. The suggestion that Yam represents the vast unruly powers of chaos is highly plausible.[11] By the conquest of Yam, Baal establishes an eternal domination over the cosmic waters with which he fertilizes the earth. The formidable character of Baal's presumptuous enemy and the ensuing authority of Baal as cosmic overlord are an integral part of this myth which has several counterparts in similar ancient Near Eastern creation and nature myths, that of Marduk versus Tiamat in the Enuma Elish being the most obvious. This prowess of Yam is then described in rather dramatic terms:[12]

ʿz ym l ymk	Yam is strong, he never yields,
l tnǧṣn pnth	His face does not quiver,
l ydlp tmnh	His countenance does not waver.[13]

Baal achieves the impossible. A mace fashioned by the heavenly blacksmiths, Kathir and Khasis, soars like an eagle in the powerful hand of Baal and deals the telling blows on the chest and forehead of Yam.[14] The role of this weapon, with its appropriate name and sympathetic power is a distinctive feature of this myth. The mace, it seems, is an object which is created especially for the destruction of Yam rather than for Baal's self-expression as the thunder god as one might assume. Above all it is the strong hand of Baal which gains the victory, the power of Baal concentrated in direct physical contact with the god of the waters.

Furthermore, the victory seems to be final. There is no obvious or explicit reference to this battle as a recurrent conflict of these gods. The issue at stake is the "eternal kingship" among the gods.

This is apparently an *ephhapax* adventure for the ultimate sovereignty of the cosmos.[15] The portentous remarks of the artisans Kathir and Khasis illustrate this fact and underscore the momentous nature of the incident:[16]

ht 'ibk b'lm	Behold your enemy, O Baal!
ht 'ibk tmḫṣ	Behold you will smite your enemy!
ht tṣmt ṣrtk	Behold you will conquer your opposition![17]
tqḥ mlk 'lmk	You will take your eternal kingdom,
drkt dt drdrk	Your everlasting dominion.[18]

The finality of the conquest also involves the total humiliation and annihilation of the enemy. The details of this action are apparent from the following translation:[19]

yqṯ b'l wyšt ym	Baal drags him forth, he scatters him![20]
ykly ṯpṭ nhr	He annihilates Judge River!
. . . .	
b'lm ymlk	Baal shall reign!

That such "dragging" and "scattering" have any ritual implications is not immediately evident. Rather, these terms emphasize the extent and nature of Yam's extermination. In the description of Pharaoh's damnation (Ezek. 29:1-5 and 32:2-8), that monarch is described as a great sea monster (*tannīn*) who is dragged from his natural habitat in the Great River and scattered across the deserts where creatures of prey will enjoy a rich repast.

The triumphant exclamations "Baal shall reign" or "Now Baal is king" are not accidental at this juncture. They fall into logical sequence and express the necessary result of the preceding action. For the kingship of Baal is totally dependent upon the victorious outcome of this conflict. Baal's kingship, unlike its human counterpart, is not hereditary; it is not designated by a vote of the pantheon. His royalty is not present because of some natural right from eternity, or by virtue of El's choice of a favorite son. It must be won by combat. And that combat, as the preceding discussion has shown, involves a rise from humiliation and servitude to glory, a herculean task to perform against a formidable foe, a victory by the might of his own hand, and the total extermination of the enemy. These are the essential features of the battle episode in the sequence involving the establishment of kingship.

The Exaltation of Baal as the Cosmic Overlord

The precise nature of the text Baal V i-vi which follows the Baal-Yam conflict cycle in the sequence of G. R. Driver,[21] is rather difficult to define. It seems preferable to take Baal V i 1 to V iii 46 as a separate unit in the sequence and to delineate its character on its own terms. There is no textual indication that Baal appears *redivivus,* as Gray assumes, for "reintegration into the living society of the active fertility powers," while any suggested reference to a *hieros gamos* is rather dubious although possible.[22] Whether the blood bath of Anat is part of a rite of imitative magic to stimulate the flow of the life essence cannot be determined with any measure of finality. It seems clear, however, that the text is concerned with the exaltation of Baal the Victor and the affirmation of his right as cosmic overlord by the expression of his creative power. That this aspect of the Baal myth may have been associated with the new season of life and fertility is plausible. The significant point at this juncture is to see this episode as a logical sequence of the Baal-Yam cycle. After the submission of chaos there follow the release of life and the creativity of the god of the cosmos.

The opening lines of the text are an exhortation to exalt Baal at a banquet in his honor. The lines read:[23]

‘bd ’al’iyn b‘l	Serve Baal the Victor,
s’id zbl b‘l ’arṣ	Exalt the Prince, Lord of the Earth!
qm yṯ‘r w’ašlḥmnh	Arise, let preparation be made, that I may dine him.

Baal is now designated as the Prince, the Victorious Lord over the earth. Such a title implies a sovereign overlordship.[24] Baal has, by virtue of his victories, become the mighty one. Thus Baal introduces his victory speech with the words: "The message of Baal the Victor, the speech of the most valiant of heroes.[25] Aliyan Baal is the victor *par excellence*. Comparable affirmations are also found in the subsequent context. Twice, for example, the following exclamation occurs:[26]

mlkn ’al’iyn b‘l	Baal the Victor is our King!
ṯpṭn w’in d ‘lnh	Our Judge, and there is none superior to him.

It is apparent that Baal is exalted as the incomparable one. He now bears the titles that once were borne by Yam, his vanquished foe, and is exalted as the Judge (*ṯpṭ*) supreme and the prince (*zbl*) over all.

The banquet in Baal’s honor soon becomes a massacre of heroes and as such a sympathetic expression of Baal’s nature as the mightiest hero of all. The slaughter ritual is performed by Anat, who is officially Baal’s sister and consort. She is also, in a certain sense, the bloodthirsty *alter ego* of Baal, the source of life and fertility. In the resultant flood of gore Anat revels triumphantly:[27]

yml’u lbh bšmḫt	Her heart is full with joy,
kbd ‘nt tšyt	The liver of Anat with victory!
kbrkm tǧll bdm ḍmr	For she plunges her knees in the blood of warriors[28]
ḥlqm bmm‘ mhrm	Her loins in the gore of heroes.

In this way the victory of Baal and his nature as the great warrior are exaggerated, while Anat represents the terrifying aspect of Baal’s role as warrior, the hypostasis of his victorious presence. Accordingly, the same catalog of mighty acts is applicable to Anat as well as to Baal. Such an array of deeds is clearly designed to overwhelm any would-be challenger. These points are illustrated by the words of Anat herself;[29]

mn ’ib yp‘ lb‘l	What enemy would rise up against Baal?[30]
ṣrt lrkb ‘rpt	What foe against the Rider of Clouds?
l mḫšt mdd ’il ym	Have I not slain Yam, beloved of El?
l klt nhr ’il rbm	Have I not annihilated the great god River?
l ’ištbm tnn ’išbmnh	Have I not muzzled Tannin, yes muzzled him?
mḫšt bṯn ‘qltn	I smote the crooked serpent!
šlyṭ d šb‘t r’ašm	The mighty one with seven heads![31]

The catalog continues in like manner, and the opening lines are repeated at the end of the speech—in the light of such mighty acts “What enemy would dare to rise up against Baal?” One gets the impression from this and similar passages that the battle motif and the dragon motif are not confined to the conquest of Yam, and that Yam and Leviathan are not identical figures. Warfare is a natural part of the existence of Baal and his consort Anat.

Whether a *hieros gamos* takes place at this point is hard to determine from the text itself, and the question remains whether just such a union is necessary before Baal can function as a creator and life-giver. In any case, to whatever various overtures of devotion on Baal's part may have reference, it is the three prominent parts of Baal's victory speech which are the arresting features of this text. The first of these is the motif of subsequent peace and wellbeing on the earth over which Baal is lord. Thus the speech begins:[32]

tḥm 'al'iyn b'l	The Message of Baal the Victor,
hwt 'al'iyn qrdm	The speech of the most valiant of heroes:[33]
qryy b'arṣ mlḥmt	"Meet me in the turbulent earth,[34]
št b'prt ddym	"Diffuse love across the land,[35]
sk šlm lkbd 'arṣ	"Pour out peace in the midst of earth
'arb dd lkbd šdm	"That I may increase love amidst the fields.[36]

After Baal has conquered the power of chaos and Anat has given complete vent to her bloodthirsty disposition, Baal invites Anat to come to the land which had been disrupted by this warfare and there exercise her function as mistress of love and fertility so that peace or well-being may again abound on the earth.

After an exhortation for Anat to hasten to his side for this purpose, Baal announces that he is about to exercise his creative activity as lord over heaven and earth. Such creative activity as an expression of victorious overlordship in no way negates the fact that the relatively inactive El is the creator god in the strict sense of the term.[37] Baal does not create heaven and earth here, either *ex nihilo* or from chaos (Yam). Rather he introduces something new into the world to demonstrate his life-giving creative power as lord of the cosmos. The pertinent lines of the text read:[38]

'abn brq dl td'šmm	I will create lightning which the heavens do not know,
rgm ltd' nšm	Thunder that mankind does not know,
wltbn hmlt 'arṣ	Nor the multitudes of the earth understand.

Such creative acts are obviously related to his character of the storm god as well, yet their presence at this point, prior to the erection of the temple from which Baal storms forth, is to be noted.

This speech of Baal concludes with an invitation to behold this new phenomenon which he has created. The rendezvous is to take place in the mountains of Ṣapon, the specially chosen abode of Baal. Finally the activity of Baal culminates in retirement to a particular sanctuary designated "the mountain of my inheritance." The relevant passage is:[39]

'atm w'ank 'ibǧyh	Come now and I will show it to you
btk ǧry 'il ṣpn	I, God of Ṣapon, in the midst of my mountain,
bqdš bǧr nḥlty	In the sanctuary, in the mountain of my inheritance,
bn'm bgb' tl'iyt	In the pleasant abode, the hill of victory.

The final expression, "hill of victory," suggests a further connection with the combat motif, this holy mountain being that which he has won—the trophy of the victorious king.

The kingship sequence is terminated at this point, even though certain of its aspects are repeated in the text which follows. In a sense this whole kingship sequence is but a prelude to the longer cycle of Baal as the storm god in which the building of a temple is involved, inasmuch as Baal cannot express his nature as storm without just such a temple-palace. This cycle will be considered in the next chapter.

In recapitulation the following pattern becomes apparent. The theme is that of Baal the warrior. He begins in ignominy and slavery, overcomes a mighty and powerful adversary by his own hand, completely annihilates his foe, and consequently gains the kingship. He is thereupon exalted as the incomparable warrior and lord of earth and exposed as a terrifying power. As king, Baal dispenses well-being on earth, exercises his creative activity, and retires to his mountain of victory. However, before Baal can exercise his kingship in the storm a temple must be built.

The Kingship of Yahweh in "The Song of the Sea"

The kingship sequence of the Baal texts has its biblical counterpart in "The Song of the Sea" (Exod. 15:1-18).[40] The present analysis of that song will delineate this sequence, make the necessary comparisons, and indicate what tentative conclusions might be drawn.

The theme of the song is the exaltation of the name and character of Yahweh as the victorious warrior. Hence its overture to worship reads:

> I will sing to Yahweh
> For He is highly exalted!
> Both horse and chariot [41]
> He hurled into the sea!
> Yahweh is a man of war!
> Yahweh is His Name! (Exod. 15:1,3)

The emphasis is clear; Yahweh is the mighty warrior, his foe the powers of Egypt, His battleground the turbulent sea (Yam). His character is demonstrated when He espouses the cause of the humiliated and downtrodden slaves of Egypt and rises to overthrow the mightiest power of that day, the army of the King of Egypt. Pharaoh is indeed a formidable foe and the victory a glorious triumph, as the subsequent lines affirm:

> The chariots and army of Pharaoh
> He cast into the sea![42]
> His crack troops
> Sank in the reed-sea!
> The deeps covered them,
> They went down to the depths as a stone!
> (Exod. 15:4-5)

The historical nature of Yahweh's adversary in no way implies his innocuous character. On the contrary the presumption and power of this god-king of Egypt is vividly reflected in the staccato lines:

> The enemy said:
> I'll pursue! I'll overtake!
> I'll divide the spoil!
> My greed will be sated!
> I'll bare my sword!
> My hand will conquer![43] (Exod. 15:9)

The victory belongs to Yahweh alone. None can withstand the

power of His right hand. This metaphor is emphasized in the following way:

> Thy right hand, O Yahweh
> Is mighty in power![44]
> Thy right hand, O Yahweh,
> Shatters the enemy! (Exod. 15:6)

Nor is this triumph a momentary or temporary act. The furious onslaught of the divine presence spells the end of the opposition, while the waters and the winds are willing agents for the total annihilation of the enemy. Thus the sea (Yam) and the storm (Baal) are but pawns of the Victor as the royal authority of Yahweh is established in the current events of history:

> In Thy great majesty
> Thou didst crush Thy foes![45]
> Thou didst send forth Thy fury,
> Thou didst blow with Thy wind,
> The sea covered them!
> They sank as lead
> In the mighty waters. (Exod. 15:7, 10)

The natural division of the song at the tenth verse corresponds in thought sequence to the division between the two sections of the Baal kingship texts described above. The first half is concerned with one aspect of the sea conflict, the battle motif. Israel and her fate are bypassed. For the moment Yahweh and Pharaoh are the only actors.

The second section opens with an explosive exaltation of Yahweh as the Incomparable One. This evaluation is based upon the mighty acts of victory He has performed. He is King in the heavens and Lord of the earth. The latter is also His battleground, His "land of warfare," and must respond to His powerful hand. The opening verses read:

> Who is like Thee among the gods, O Yahweh?
> Who is like Thee, mighty among the holy ones?[46]
> Awesome in laudable deeds,
> Performer of great feats!
> Thou didst extend Thy right hand,
> The earth swallowed them.[47] (Exod. 15:11f.)

A further consequence of the victorious combat is the revelation of the terrifying reality of the divine presence. All prospective foes are paralyzed by the *'ēmā* of Yahweh[48] and the nature of Yahweh as a true "man of war" is thereby acknowledged. None can gainsay the petrifying terror of His militant character. Thus, after relating how the princes of Philistia, Moab, Edom, and Canaan reacted to this overwhelming presence of Yahweh, the climax reads:

> Terror and dread overcame them,
> In the greatness of Thy arm
> They were struck dumb as a stone.
> Till Thy people pass over, O Yahweh,
> Till the people Thou hast created pass over.
> (Exod. 15:16)

Here the vicarious nature of this victory becomes evident! Yahweh is fighting for His people, they are His redeemed (v. 13) and more especially his creation. [49] Hence the creative activity of Yahweh as King is illustrated by the molding of a new people. Israel is indeed "what God has wrought" (Num. 23:23).

The description of the final action of Yahweh, in which He retires to His holy mountain, reflects an imagery quite similar to that of its counterpart in the Baal texts. This glorious finale is anticipated earlier in the strophe:

> Thou didst faithfully lead them,
> The people whom Thou didst redeem
> Thou didst guide them by Thy might,
> To Thy holy encampment. (Exod. 15:13)

The precise location of the holy encampment (*nẹwē qodšekā*) is vigorously disputed. Canaan and Zion are the alternatives proposed. The term encampment is in itself a neutral concept applicable to Canaan, Zion, and Yahweh Himself.[50] The subsequent portrait of this location is even more colorful:

> Thou wilt bring them and plant them,
> In the mountain of thy heritage.
> Thou hast made, O Yahweh
> The place of Thy rule,
> The sanctuary, O Yahweh
> Thy hands have established. (Exod. 15:17)

In Baal V iii 44-46, discussed above, the abode of Baal is described both as a sanctuary (*qdš*) and as the "mountain of my heritage" (*ǧr nḥlty*) a description which precedes the building of the temple for Baal. Thus the "mountain of heritage" seems to refer to the chosen divine abode and not to a specific temple locality. Elsewhere the throne (*ks'u ṯbt*) of Mot is apparently identical with his domain (*'rṣ nḥlt*).[51] Likewise, the abode of Yahweh where Israel is "planted" is not necessarily confined to Mount Zion but is, in the first instance, applicable to Canaan as Yahweh's personal inheritance.[52] Canaan is His throne. However, just as in the Baal sequence a palace or temple constructed as a symbol of the royal abode is naturally associated with the reign of the god, so too the sanctuary made or established by Yahweh would readily be connected with the rule of Yahweh from His central sanctuary.

In view of this sequence depicting Yahweh as the Warrior without peer, who espouses the cause of the enslaved, rises to conquer Pharaoh His mighty adversary with His own right hand, completely annihilates His foe, receives fitting exaltation as the supreme God, reveals to all His terrible presence, and reaches the holy mountain from which He rules—the final verse is apropos indeed. For just as Baal receives an eternal kingship thereby (Baal III* A 10), Yahweh too "will reign for ever and ever" (Exod. 15:18).

The Relevance of the Battle for Kingship Motif

What conclusions can be drawn from the preceding comparison and what contributions can be made for a deeper appreciation of biblical thought? In the first place, the thought sequence in the respective battles for divine kingship is remarkably similar. In several cases the same terminology is employed. In other cases the biblical concepts are elucidated by their Canaanite equivalents. Although none of these facts demonstrate any direct literary dependency, they do suggest that the concept of divine kingship had associated with it a cycle of ideas also current within Canaanite circles, and that the biblical writer in describing the exodus event either consciously or unconsciously employed this sequence in order to emphasize the kingship of Yahweh. Whether this presents a conscious and direct polemic against Baal is not clear, despite the numerous striking antitheses. In any case the archaic character of the kingship motif as an integral part of the covenant faith of Israel can no longer be dismissed. This statement is also confirmed by recent investigations into the precise nature of the covenant as a mutual agreement patterned after the archaic suzerainty treaties between King and vassals.[53] In the covenant Yahweh is acknowledged as King (Deut. 33:5):

> Yahweh became King in Jeshurun,
> When the heads of the people were gathered,
> The tribes of Israel together. (Deut. 33:5)

As the warrior in Israel's midst, Yahweh's royal power becomes manifest (Num. 23:21f.). In other words, these and similar references confirm the major significance of the Kingship of Yahweh in the Israelite covenant and in early Hebrew poetry.[54]

However, when one makes a detailed analysis of the nature of the exploits of Baal and the *magnalia* of Yahweh one becomes aware of a pronounced tension between the two. For while both Baal and Yahweh appear as mighty and triumphant warriors who exhibit both destructive and creative powers beyond compare, their feats are presented from different frames of reference. Baal's activity is an epic among gods, a cosmological and mythical encounter. Yahweh's revelation of his kingship involves a definable locality in time and space, a historical opponent, and a local world power. Sea (Yam), wind (Baal), and kindred natural forces are obedient servants and not personified chaotic foes.

Moreover, apart from Baal's inevitable involvement in the well-being of the earth by the dispensation of fertility, there is no indication of his concern for a specific people, no sovereign choice of one people over another. Nature and not people is his concern. His "experiment in love" is in the kissing of earth with peace and well-being, his communion is with Anat, his holiness in the numinous isolation of his mountain in the North. Any indication of an election motif is totally absent. Divine wrath and jealousy have no direct connection with any designated people. The elimination of rivals and the bloody exploits of his *alter ego* are but the expression of Baal's character in cosmic affairs without any direct relevance to a sensitive pathos over against a particular nation.

The relevance of this comparison is not only antithetical. For the Israelite who had come into contact with Canaanite culture, and in particular with Canaanite mythology, would have been aware that divine kingship was popularly considered something that had to be won, not simply inherited, inherent, or given.[55] Hence, it is quite plausible that in such a milieu the proclamation of the victorious acts of warfare on the part of Yahweh would be an emphatic way of affirming the divine kingship of Yahweh. Such an affirmation would automatically sound certain polemical overtones. Moreover it is precisely these royal acts of triumph which provide the impetus for Israel's response to Yahweh as the king and overlord in the covenant. Wherever Yahweh intervened to defeat the enemy of Israel He was reasserting His Kingship, which also means that the battle motif was an inevitable part of the concept of divine kingship so prevalent in the subsequent worship of Israel.[56]

If the presence of certain Canaanite divine kingship imagery in "The Song of the Sea" be granted, then the wording of Exod. 15:11 and similar passages is more readily understood. In the first place the assertion, "Who is like Thee among the gods, O Yahweh?" is dependent upon the subsequent proclamation of His performance of victorious acts. Such an assertion, however, says nothing explicitly concerning the essential existence of other gods as such; it simply employs the common Canaanite image of divine kingship as an "established superiority over all gods" in relation to Yahweh Himself.[57] In other words, this is a culturally relevant way of saying Yahweh, not Baal, is King. And as the context shows, Yahweh is King in Israel; Israel is His creation and Canaan His heritage. By acknowledging Yahweh as its own King, Israel is affirming the direct unmediated divine rule of Yahweh in its own midst and not merely in some heavenly council of gods.

If this battle motif is relevant in a general way, then those later biblical passages which speak of combatants explicitly mentioned in the Ugaritic texts cannot be ignored either. Tannin, for example, is used as a metaphor to describe Pharaoh who is given the "scattering treatment" applied to Yam (Ezek. 29:3-5) and made a torrent of blood that would delight the heart of Anat (Ezek. 29:1-8). Not only is the "battle for kingship" imagery applied to the exodus event, but Pharaoh, the foe *par excellence*, is described in terms of the mythological dragons enumerated among the mighty acts in Baal's rise to kingship. Yet the enemy of Yahweh is still Pharaoh! This fact becomes even clearer in Isa. 51:9-11, where the same victorious arm of Yahweh, who once divided the sea, hewed Rahab, and pierced Tannin for the redeemed to pass over, is now called into action to bring the redeemed once more to its mountain of rest![58] In the context Tannin and Rahab logically refer to Pharaoh, the mightiest of Yahweh's historical foes.[59] In Ps. 74:12-14 the psalmist, after defining his current predicament amid vicious foes, recalls the revelation of Yahweh's divine kingship in His past conquests:

> Yet God is my King from of old,
> Performing *salvation* in the midst of earth,
> Thou didst divide the sea (Yam) with Thy might,
> Thou didst break the heads of Tannin upon the waters,
> Thou didst crush the heads of Leviathan,
> Thou didst give him as food for a people among desert creatures

In the light of the preceding, this divine act of salvation on earth is apparently the exodus event, the division of the sea is the parting of the waters at the Reed Sea, while Tannin and Leviathan are once again the mighty Pharaoh as well as Egypt for which he stands. If this line of thinking is correct, then, to this point there is no reference to an independent mythological battle between Yahweh and a dragon, but simply the application of the Canaanite "battle for kingship" imagery to the revelation of Yahweh's kingship in the glorious exodus battle. And, as W. Schmidt has demonstrated, the conflict between Baal and the dragons, whether Yam, Leviathan, Tannin, or Bathan, is not directly connected with the creation of the cosmos as such.[60] In other words a dragon myth is not necessarily a creation myth. The Babylonian myth of Marduk and Tiamat may be the exception rather than the rule. It is incorrect then, as some have done, to state that biblical dragon imagery is always the relic of an ancient creation myth, for in the passages noted above the conflicts involved all take place after creation, the dragon imagery being applied to the battles of time and history.

Can the same statement be made concerning the biblical references to Yahweh's conflict with the sea (Yam)? It is clear that in "The Song of the Sea" (Exod. 15) the sea itself is in no way personified![61] And again, as noted above, there is no indication that the Baal-Yam encounter involves a creation or cosmogony in the strict sense of the term. It is the battle for cosmic control of the created world.

While it is true that the vast majority of biblical allusions to *yam* speak of the sea as such, there are certain passages which suggest that *yam* and *mayīm* (*rabbīm*) represent something more.[62] The sea is first of all a divine creation, "The sea is His and He made it" (Ps. 95:5); it is the very foundation of the Lord's earth (Ps. 24:1f.). The sea and the waters are in fact a regular feature of the creation portrait in the Old Testament, but without any explicit description of a battle which took place before creation. In His creative acts the waters simply flee at His coming (Ps. 104:5-9). Nevertheless, such waters do appear to become presumptuous and menacing at times (Ps. 46:2f.) and the worshiper often describes his plight in relation to the sea's rebellious activity.[63] But no battle takes place; Yahweh always has these powers under control. Above all the tumult of the roaring sea Yahweh reigns as King (Ps. 93:1-4). In a general way the sea does represent the chaotic and catastrophic phenomena observable in nature, yet there is no evidence of Yahweh having fought the sea for supremacy on earth. Accordingly, the description of Yahweh as the King who establishes His throne upon the flood or reigns over the sea is a culturally relevant way of saying that Yahweh, not Baal, is King over all cosmic forces. Nor is it surprising that, despite the completely impersonal character of *yam* in Exod. 15:1-18, other exodus passages which characterize Egypt as Rahab, Leviathan, or Tannin, should complete the picture and speak of the sea in a way which suggests the Yam-Baal imagery,[64] and thereby emphasize the cosmic kingship of Yahweh. Yahweh reigns supreme as Lord of both historical and chaotic powers—the victor over all. Does this also mean that Yahweh is Lord of the Storm in the same sense that Baal is? This question is the burden of the next chapter.

NOTES

[1] The name Aliyan is derived from the root *l'y* (Accadian *le'ū*, Hebrew *la'ah*), meaning "to prevail." See Gordon, *Ugaritic Manual*, p. 283.

[2] The first cycle of the kingship texts consists of (VI ii-iv;) III* C, B, A found in G. R. Driver, *Canaanite Myths and Legends* pp. 73-83. These texts are numbered 129, 137, and 68 in the manual of Gordon, *Ugaritic Manual*, pp. 160, 168, 150.

[3] The second kingship text treated in this chapter is Baal V i 1 to V iii 46, text number Anat I 1 - III 28 in Gordon, *Ugaritic Manual*, pp. 187f.

[4] For a discussion of this problem see Kapelrud, *Baal in the Ras Shamra Texts*, pp. 13-27. Gray, *The Legacy of Canaan*, p. 11 stresses the functional character of these texts. Compare the very cautious remarks of R. de Langhe, "Myth, Ritual and Kingship in the Ras Shamra Tablets," Myth, Ritual and Kingship, ed. by S. Hooke (Oxford: Clarendon Press, 1958), p. 141, who concludes, "The existence of these 'dramatic performances' needs to be proved, otherwise than by the presence of the cycle in question."

[5] Baal VI iv 14f. is the only place where this name appears. The identification of YW with YHW(H) in the Old Testament is highly improbable. Although Yahweh is sometimes written YW, the characters of the two deities are quite incompatible. See Gray, *The Legacy of Canaan*, pp. 133f. Note also the subsequent assertion of R. Dussaud, "Yahweh fils de El," *Syria*, XXXIV (1957), 237, who uses this reference to support his contention that Yahweh (equals YW) is depicted as the son of El in Old Testament passages such as Deut. 32:8f.

[6] Baal III* B 16-17.

[7] The Arabic *waqā* "keep, protect" provides a plausible parallel. See G. Driver, p. 165; Gray, p. 22.

[8] Compare the Hebrew *hạmullā*, Jer. 11:16; Ezek. 1:24.

[9] There is no need to discard the original suggestion of Gordon, p. 312, that *pḏ* means "gold," and to appeal to Egyptian loan word parallels as G. R. Driver, *Canaanite Myths and Legends*, p. 163 and Gray, *Legacy of Canaan*, p. 22 have done. The Hebrew *paz*, is etymologically related, and Yam's demand for Baal's gold is paralleled by Baal's acquisition of gold (*ḫrṣ*) from his victorious exploits in Baal V iii 61f.

[10] Baal III* B 34-35.

[11] Thus de Langhe, "Myth, Ritual, and Kingship," p. 138, Gray, *The Legacy of Canaan*, pp. 9f., and numerous other scholars.

[12] Baal III* A 17.

[13] For a comparable meaning of the roots *mkk* and *dlp* as "yield, weaken, sink" and "sag, give way, waver" respectively, see Eccles. 10:18, "Through sloth the roof sinks in, and through indolence the house gives way." Further it seems preferable to connect *pnt* with the Accadian *pānātu*, "front" as done by G. R. Driver, *Canaanite Myths and Legends*, p. 163, and *tmn* with the Hebrew *tẹmūnā* "likeness, form or appearance."

[14] The term "chest" renders the Ugaritic *bn ydm*, literally "between two hands"; cf. Zech. 13:6. "Forehead" renders *bn'nm* literally "between two eyes" as in Deut. 6:8; 11:18.

[15] "Jedenfalls wird eine Königherrschaft verheissen, die zu einer bestimmten Zeit (eben mit dem Sieg über Jam) ihren Anfang nimmt und für die Zukunft unabänderlich ist," concludes W. Schmidt, *Königtum Gottes in Ugarit und Israel* (Berlin: Alfred Töpelmann, 1961), p. 43. From Aqhat I i 44f. it appears that Baal is indeed lord over the great cosmic deep (*thmtm*).

[16] Baal III* A 8-10.

[17] For the use of *ṣmt* in the sense of annihilation of a foe see Pss. 54:7; 73:27; 94:23; 143:12.

[18] For the concept of "power" associated with the root *drk* see Hos. 10:11; Prov. 31:3; for the concept of "dominion" or "powerful rule" see Deut. 32:4; Ps. 77:14, 138:4f. For a discussion of the remarkable parallelism between the last two lines of this quotation and Ps. 145:13 see N. Schmidt, *The Jewish New Year Festival*, pp. 44f.; cf. also Dan. 3:33; 4:31; Exod. 15:18.

[19] Baal III* A 27, 32.

[20] Note the Arabic parallels cited by Gray, *The Legacy of Canaan*, p. 25. Cf. J. Obermann, "How Baal Destroyed a Rival," *Journal of the American Oriental Society*, LXVII (1947), 195-201.

[21] G. R. Driver, *Canaanite Myths and Legends*, pp. 82-91.

[22] Gray, *The Legacy of Canaan*, p. 32, 36f.

[23] Baal V i 2-5. The root *s'd* is parallel with *kbd* in Aqhat II v 29 which suggests the translation "exalt."

[24] There are no chthonic associations connected with this title as Kapelrud, *Baal in the Ras Shamra Texts*, pp. 60f., seems to imply.

[25] Baal V iii 29f.

[26] Baal V v 32f.; II iv 43f. Kapelrud, *Baal in the Ras Shamra Texts*, pp. 63f. observes that "the final sentence must be a hint intended to hit El, who was supposed to be the supreme head of the pantheon," and to whom this exclamation was directed. Cf. W. Schmidt, *Königtum Gottes in Ugarit und Israel*, pp. 27f.

[27] Baal V ii 25-29.

[28] For the meaning of *ḍmr* compare the Arabic parallel *ḍamīr* "brave"; see Gordon, *Ugaritic Manual*, p. 257.

[29] Baal V iii 52-58. Note the parallel passage in Baal I* i 1-4 which is treated by W. Albright, "Are the Ephod and Teraphim mentioned in the Ugaritic Literature?" *Bulletin of the American Schools of Oriental Research*, LXXXIII (1941), 39-42.

[30] The use of the root *yp'* in Ugaritic as meaning "rise up," "challenge," "be presumptuous," is significant for an appreciation of certain Old Testament texts such as Ezek. 28:17; Deut. 33:2; Pss. 50:2; 80:2; 94:1. See further T. Gaster, "Ezekiel XXVIII:17," *Expository Times*, LXII, (1950) 124, and F. L. Moriarty, "A note on *yp'*," *Catholic Biblical Quarterly*, XIV (1952), 62.

[31] For Old Testament references to Tannin, Leviathan and the dragon

motif see "The Relevance of the Battle for Kingship Motif," later in this chapter.

32 Baal V iii 28-32.

33 Albright, *Archeology and the Religion of Israel*, p. 195, translates the second and third lines, "I prevail over the heroes who meet me in the land of battle." For *qrdm* see Accadian *quradu* "hero." The difficulty with Albright's translation is that the preceding *hwt* seems to be isolated without a grammatical dependent. Cf. Gray, *The Legacy of Canaan*, p. 122.

34 *Qryy* "meet me" agrees perfectly with line 34 below, "May your feet run to me." The translation of *mlḥmt* as "unions" seems rather forced and unnecessary; See Gray, *The Legacy of Canaan*, p. 37. The obvious reading "land of warfare" as a reference to what has just preceded is quite logical.

35 *Ddym* suggests Hebrew *dōdîm* "love."

36 Gordon, *Ugaritic Manual*, p. 242, reads *'arbdd* as one word, G. R. Driver,*Canaanite Myths and Legends*, p. 87 translates "honey from a pot," and Gray, *The Legacy of Canaan*, p. 37 has "increase love." The transition to the first person "I will increase love," is supported by a similar transition in the subsequent lines of Baal V iii 35-40. Cf. A. Goetze, "Peace on Earth," *Bulletin of the American Schools of Oriental Research*, XCIII (1944), 17-20.

37 M. Pope, *El in the Ugaritic Texts*, pp. 49f. Note the distinction of W. Schmidt, *Königtum Gottes in Ugarit und Israel*, p. 50, "Während El der Schöpfer ist, begegnet in Baal der Erhalter der Schöpfung."

38 Baal V iii 41-43. *Rgm* is here translated on the basis of the Accadian *rigmu* "speech, roaring, noise," (cf. Ps. 68:28), although the normal meaning in Ugaritic is "word." The Hebrew *regem* "stone" may suggest "hailstone" as another possibility.

39 Baal V iii 43-46. The present translation follows Gray, *The Legacy of Canaan*, p. 38, in the main.

40 For the treatment of the archaic features of this song see Cross and Freedman, "The Song of Miriam," 237-50. Other recent treatments of the song include those of H. Schmidt, "Das Meerlied," *Zeitschrift für die alttestamentliche Wissenschaft*, XLIX (1931), 59-66; M. Rozelaar, "The Song of the Sea," *Vetus Testamentum*, II (1952), 221-28; J. D. Watts, "The Song of the Sea," *Vetus Testamentum*, VII (1957), 371-80; cf. T. Gaster, "Notes on the Song of the Sea," *The Expository Times*, XLVIII (1936-37), 45.

41 The vocalization *rekeb* "chariot" is plausible and supported by the present stage of archeological and historical investigation into the date of the introduction of cavalry, Cross and Freedman, "The Song of Miriam," p. 243.

42 The meaning of *yry* in Ugaritic as "go forth" or "go down" (as in Baal IV ii 11, 29f.; I* i 6) would suggest the translation, "They went down into the sea." The use of *yrd* in v. 5 supports this translation. Cf. G. R. Driver, "Hebrew Notes," *Vetus Testamentum*, I (1951), 249f.

43 Cross and Freedman, "The Song of Miriam," p. 246, agree that the verbs "stated" and "conquer" (originally *tml'm and trsm*) preserve the archaic enclitic mem. Hence the translation given here.

44 The meaning of "mighty" or "strong" is suggested by the Ugaritic *'dr*. For the various translations of *'dr* see Gray, *The Legacy of Canaan*, p. 78.

45 Note the use of *ga'anu* and the participle *qāmu* in Aqhat II vi 43 and Baal IV ii 25 respectively.

46 The rendering "holy ones" is supported by the Septuagint. Note also

the parallelism with *'ēlîm*, and the frequent reference to holy ones in the Ugaritic texts. See, for example, Baal III* B 18f., "the gods sat down to food, the holy ones to a meal." For *'ēlîm* in the Old Testament see Pss. 29:1; 89:7; Deut. 32:8. The "holy ones" are suggested in Deut. 32:2; Ps. 89:6-8; Zech. 14:5, *et passim*. See further Cross and Freedman, "The Blessing of Moses," 201.

47 Cross and Freedman, "The Song of Miriam," p. 247, have suggested that *'ereṣ* is here personified and represents the underworld. If so, a polemic against Baal who must descend into the underworld (*'rṣ*) of Mot may be implied. Cross and Freedman refer to Isa. 29:4; Gen. 2:6; Isa. 14:9; Jonah 2:7 and other passages to illustrate their point.

48 See Ch. II, n. 28.

49 For the meaning of *qnh* as "create" or "beget" See Chapter II, n. 22.

50 For the use of the term in reference to Yahweh see Jer. 50:7; in reference to Zion, Isa. 33:20; in reference to Canaan or Israel, Jer. 10:25; Isa. 32:18; Ps. 79:7; Jer. 31:23. For the use of the term in the Mari documents, see Cross and Freedman, "The Song of Miriam," p. 244.

51 Baal I* ii 15f.; II viii 13f.

52 One cannot ignore that Sinai was also considered a holy mountain (Exod. 19:4; 24:13; Judg. 5:5; Deut. 33:1; I Kings 19:8). Watts, "The Song of the Sea," p. 378 maintains that Jerusalem alone can be meant here. For the opposite view, see Cross and Freedman, "The Song of Miriam," pp. 240, 250. For Canaan (Israel) as Yahweh's inheritance see Jer. 2:7; 12:8f.; 16:18; 50:11.

53 Compare the treatment in Ch. I.

54 See also Num. 10:35; Judg. 8:23; I Sam. 4:4; 8:7; 12:12; Pss. 24:9; 68:25. In recent times the same conclusion has been reached by Cross and Freedman, "The Song of Miriam," p. 250 and E. Jacob, *Ras Shamra et l'ancien Testament* (Neuchatel: Delachaux & Niestle, 1960), p. 88. Compare also the discussion of W. Schmidt, *Königtum Gottes in Ugarit und Israel*, pp. 64-69, who insists that the entry into Canaan is the *terminus a quo* for this concept.

55 *Supra*, p. 54.

56 See J. Gray, "The Kingship of God in the Prophets and Psalms," *Vetus Testamentum*, XI (1961), 1-29. Note especially Pss. 47, 95, 99, which associate Yahweh's Kingship solely with Exodus themes.

57 For a discussion of the role of "Yahweh als König der Götter," see W. Schmidt, *Königtum Gottes in Ugarit und Israel*, pp. 69-76. The subject will be discussed in greater detail in a later chapter.

58 The similarity in terminology between this passage and Exod. 15 is immediately apparent.

59 In Ps. 87:4 and Isa. 30:7 Rahab is clearly identified with Egypt which would support the identification of the same in Ps. 89:11. Just as in Exod. 15:11 Yahweh is here exalted as the incomparable One because of His control of the sea and conquest of Rahab and all His foes. Cf. also Job 9:13; 26:12.

60 W. Schmidt, *Königtum Gottes in Ugarit und Israel*, pp. 39-42.

61 Cross and Freedman, "The Song of Miriam," p. 239.

62 See H. G. May, "Some Cosmic Connotations of *Mayim Rabbim*, 'Many Waters'," *Journal of Biblical Literature*, LXXIV (1955), 9-21, for a somewhat extreme position on the subject.

63 Pss. 42:8; 69:2f., 16f.; 124:4f.; 144:7; 68:22f.; 89:26.

[64] Isa. 43:15-17; Pss. 74:12-15; 89:9f.; Job 25:12. There is much of the Baal-Yam imagery suggested in Hab. 3. See especially, Albright, "The Psalm of Habakkuk," pp. 1-18. This passage will be discussed in the next chapter.

Chapter IV

THE THEOPHANY OF BAAL AND THE THEOPHANY OF YAHWEH

If the current comparison of religious imagery from kindred cultures is a somewhat precarious adventure, then the subsequent effort to establish the distinctive characteristics of pertinent religious concepts of the Old Testament in every nuance of meaning is fraught with similar dangers. The presence of a concept within the covers of the Old Testament in no way demands that this concept is distinctive in every detail. The concept of the theophany of Yahweh in early Hebrew poetry is a particular case in point. This chapter is devoted to a consideration of the spectacular self-manifestation of Baal and comparable theophanies of Yahweh which illustrate the problem involved.[1] In such a study the question of similarity and perspective becomes especially relevant for an appreciation of the religious polemic of Israel in its struggle for religious self-preservation within the mesh of Canaanite society.

The Character of Baal as the Storm God

The Baal of the Ugaritic pantheon is none other than the ancient semitic storm god Hadad. He is so named in the texts themselves and as such he appears as the victorious king in the Canaanite council of gods. Hadad is *the* Baal of Canaan![12] The dramatic portrait of Baal on a stele found at Ugarit offers a vivid character sketch.[3] Baal stands erect as a vigorous young warrior god, brandishing a club in one hand and holding a lightning flash which culminates in a huge spear head in the other. Beneath the feet of Baal, it seems, are turbulent waves which represent the sea or the flood over which Baal is victorious.

As the storm god Baal bears the distinctive title "the rider of the clouds" (*rkb ʿrpt*).[4] This colorful expression underscores the Canaanite belief that the presence of Baal was evident from the advent of nimbus clouds in the heavens. These are, as it were, the "chariots" of Baal (cf. Ps. 104:3). Thunder and lightning are his weapons, and the mountains of the North are the fortress from which he charges forth. As mentioned earlier, thunder and lightning are Baal's own creation, the personal expression of his victorious overlordship, his supremacy, and his individuality as the storm god becomes king. The pertinent text was previously translated:[5]

> I will create lightning which the heavens do not know,
> Thunder that mankind does not know,
> Nor the multitudes[6] of the earth understand.

Baal's theophany in the storm is a revelation of his powerful control over all the waters of heaven with which he renders fertile his earthly domain. Baal's very existence is bound up with the forces of the storm, the repeated revelation of which, in some such heavenly spectacle, is the *sine qua non* of his being alive. When at a later period Baal must descend into the underworld, he is obliged to take his clouds (*ʿrpt*), wind (*rḥ*) and rain (*mṭr*), the absence of which, in the eyes of the worshipers in Canaan, was an indication of his death.[7]

It is characteristic of Baal as the storm god that the divine self-disclosure of his being in the phenomena of natural forces is not effected in isolation from other deities. Not only is Baal intent upon demonstrating his kingship in the weather to the anxious council of the heavens, but he is frequently associated with a retinue of holy ones who are, apparently, lesser manifestations of his presence. The recurring names of the holy ones are "Pdry daughter of mist," "Tly daughter of showers," and "'Arṣy daughter of Yʿbdr."[8] Some such lackeys of Baal are also included in Yam's demands to the heavenly council.[9] In his northern abode this heavenly monarch enjoys the company of his daughters and invites his wife Anat, the first lady of fertility, to share his quarters.[10] This company of Baal, it seems, is necessary for his dispensation of life in the elements of nature.

Although Baal, as the storm god is king among gods, and although strong lesser deities are always at his side, Baal does not possess an independent and unrestricted power of the theophany in the storm. Baal's victory over Yam for the kingship is laughable if he cannot exercise his powers of kingship on the weather or function as the victorious one by a vigorous self-expression in the realms of his domain. And laughable it is until a further prerequisite is fulfilled. For, strange to say, the rider of the storm clouds requires the confines of a particular heavenly structure within which to operate effectively as a king in the forces of the storm.

The Theophany of Baal from his Temple

The absence of a fitting house for King Baal evokes the ire of Anat, his bride, who threatens to let her bloodthirsty fury loose upon the aged El residing far off in the two rivers.[11] Her bloody invectives are apparently without effect, however, for trickery is thereupon employed with much greater success. Athirat (Asherah), El's wife, is bribed with an appropriate gift of royal furniture constructed by the heavenly blacksmiths and induced to obtain El's permission for the erection of Baal's house.[12] To be without such a palace meant ignominy and humiliation in the eyes of his fellow gods, as Baal himself recounts:[13]

y‘n ’ali’yn b‘l	Baal, the Victor, answered,
yt’dd rkb ‘rpt	The rider of the clouds repeated,
hm ydd wyqlṣn	Behold, they draw back[14] and insult me,[15]
ydm wywpṯn	They rise up and spit on me,
btk p(ḫ)r bn ’ilm	In the midst of the assembly of the sons of El.

It is clear therefore that Baal's authority is limited and that El must grant permission before the house of Baal can be built and theophany take place. Once the "Lady of the Sea," Athirat, has softened the heart of her aged consort El and gained the desired approval for the project she indicates the full significance of the forthcoming building:[16]

wn 'ap ʻdn mṭrh b'l y'dn	Now, moreover, Baal will give an abundance of his rain,
ʻdn ŧrt bglŧ	An abundance of moisture and snow,
w(y)tn qlh b'rpt	He will utter his voice in the clouds,
šrh l'arṣ brqm	His flashing to the earth with lightning!

These lines make it clear that the self-disclosure of Baal is associated with excessive rain (or snow), thunder, clouds, fire and lightning, and that this theophany is intimately connected with a specific house which is variously designated *bt* (house), *hkl* (palace or temple), or *bhtm* (mansion). The location of this house is apparently in the distant mountains of the North, for it is thither that Anat hastens with the news of El's approval, and where the work of construction begins with suitable timber from Lebanon and Sirion (cf. Ps. 29:6).[17] The enormous size and beauty of the temple suggest that this is not some earthly temple which is under construction but a palace which may be a portion of the heavens themselves, presumably somewhere on the Northern horizon, from which Baal proceeds in meteorological splendor.

Two points need to be emphasized: Baal's theophany as the storm god is apparent from the spectacular weather phenomena in the heavens above and the temple of Baal is that specific location of the heavens from which this royal self-expression emanates. Thus, to that extent, the terms "temple" and "heavens" can be considered parallel. In brief, a heavenly residential palace, a location for the exercise of kingship in cosmic proportions, and not merely some earthly shrine, appear to be the nature of this *hkl*.

On the surface there is no apparent reason for Baal's objection to a window which the heavenly architects have proposed for this temple of Baal. A number of scholars, such as U. Cassuto,[18] relate this to the incipient conflict between Baal and Mot and connect it with a suggested allusion in Jer. 9:20. A more plausible explanation is that Baal, as lord of the seasons, is obliged to wait until the appropriate time before he permits the seasonal rains to fall.[19] At that time the window in question could be inserted and the spectacle of his advent be seen.

The window in question is the point of departure for Baal's appearance in the storm and the heavenly exit for the elements which must accompany the storm god. The opening of the window means the opening of the clouds through which the rain can fall. The relevant passage reads:[20]

ypth hln bbhtm	He will open a window in the mansion,
'urbt bqrb hklm	A shutter[21] in the midst of the palace,
wy(p)th bdqt 'rpt	He will make an opening in the clouds.

T. Gaster may well be right in considering this incident a reflection of an actual rain-making ceremony at the Baal temple of Ugarit, in which the windows of the temple roof or the skylight were flung open as a sympathetic gesture to induce rain.[22] In response Baal would open the flood gates of his heavenly temple and make the necessary opening in the clouds for the precipitation of rain. In any case the window of heaven or the heavenly temple is a further prerequisite for Baal's complete self-revelation as the god of the storm who brings lifegiving rain.

The building of this temple or palace is celebrated with a joyous banquet to which all the seventy sons of Athirat are invited.[23] The window is then constructed in the palace, and Baal thunders forth his stentorian voice in open challenge to all his foes. In that moment the theophany of Baal is seen. Unfortunately, some of the details of his meteorological activity are obscure because of the poor state of the text at this point. Nevertheless, it is clear that Baal thunders triumphantly, "he utters his holy voice" (*qlh qdš ytn*), his awful presence causes considerable agitation in the high places of the earth (*bmt 'arṣ*), his foes flee to the deep recesses of the forest, and he waves his spear (literally "cedar") victoriously in his right hand as lightning bolts rend the skies.[24] It is apparent that the theophany of Baal is designed to terrify his opponents and to express his complete kingship and lordship over all. The storm god is king *de facto;* he has finally given full expression to his individuality as the victorious storm god. At that moment Baal's theophany is a demonstration of his divine supremacy and a disclosure of his essential nature. The full force of his efficacious kingship is brought out in the subsequent text:[25]

bkm yṯb b'l lbhth	Henceforth Baal sits [enthroned] over his mansion!
'u mlk 'u bl mlk	Shall king or commoner
'arṣ drkt yštkn	Make the earth a dominion for himself?

Baal is enthroned as king and by virtue of his theophany must now be acknowledged as such.

The Temple Cultus of Baal as Storm God

One conspicuous feature of the preceding Baal cycle is not merely that Baal is a "king without a castle," that is, a god without a temple, but that he is the only one of the Canaanite pantheon in this predicament, a fact which occasions taunts and derision from the remainder of the gods. Marduk, on the other hand, is the first to be housed according to Babylonian mythology.[26] The suggestion that behind this myth can be seen the historical process of Baal's introduction into the Canaanite pantheon, and that Baal is thus portrayed as the founder of a new cult, is indeed plausible. One thing at least is clear: Baal is not only portrayed as a young god[27] but appears as a new god with newly acquired kingship in the Canaanite pantheon, whereas El, the titular head, is an aged figure.

It is logical to assume that, just as the various portrayals of El, Baal, Anat, and other Canaanite deities on stone or some other medium correspond to their character in the various known myths concerning them, so the temple of Baal discovered at Ugarit was considered a replica of its heavenly archetype.[28]

Some rain-making ceremony of a sympathetic nature corresponding to the opening of the windows in the heavenly temple of the Baal myth was probably performed in the Baal temple at Ugarit. If so, then in the mind of the Caananite worshiper, the self -revelation of Baal was neither an independent act nor a sovereign intervention, all of which exposes a character trait comparable to the inefficacy of Baal prior to El's gracious permission to build a royal temple. In any case, the temple of Baal is a *sine qua non* for his efficacy, even though the specific rites in the earthly ceremonies which were thought to effect Baal's revelation are relatively obscure. In the last analysis, the Canaanite could not consider a Baal theophany a sovereign act free from cultic involvement.

At this point it ought to be mentioned that the precise nature of the sacrificial system and cultic rituals at Ugarit is far from clear.[29] In general, however, it would appear that sacrifices and similar ritual activities were meant to influence the god or gods in one way or another, either by plying them with food or honoring them with gifts.[30] This function seems quite clear in Keret I iii-iv where Keret reacts to the appearance of El in a dream by ascending the tower of his palace to implore the aid of El and effect the assistance of Baal in his forthcoming venture in search of a suitable wife:[31]

w'ly lẓr mgdl	Then he went up to the top of the tower,
rkb ŧkmm ḥmt	He mounted the shoulder of the wall,
nš'a ydh šmmh	He raised his hands to the sky,
dbḥ lŧr 'abh 'il	He sacrificed to bull El, his father,
šrd b'l bdbḥh	He made Baal descend with this sacrifice,
bn dgn bmṣdh	The son of Dagan with his food.

One cannot press the term *šrd* into meaning that Keret actually induced a theophany.[32] However, the thought that he invoked and effected divine aid seems clear from the context. Likewise, when Keret arrived at the shrine of Athirat, his vow of ample gifts of silver and gold gained him the support of that deity also.[33] That certain of these rites were sympathetic in nature cannot be denied, but that the entire myth of Baal's theophany in the storm was reenacted in a ritual drama at the annual New Year Festival is nowhere specified, nor can the details of such a drama be clearly discerned from the pattern of the myth itself.[34] This does not rule out the fact that many features of the Baal myth correspond to similar ancient Near Eastern myths with attendant rituals. It is not possible to enter into the controversy concerning the myth-ritual problem in ancient mythology at this time.[35] Suffice it to say that any attempt to find the origins of Hebrew cultic practices or the ritual for a corresponding Hebrew myth-ritual pattern in the Baal myth has very little explicit textual evidence for its support.

The Theophanies of Yahweh in the Early Israelite Poetry

To what extent is the mythological portrait of Baal's storm theophany the same as comparable descriptions of Yahweh's advent in nature? Is there any indication that biblical writers employed this Canaanite imagery for a specific purpose? In what way is Yahweh's theophanic self-revelation distinctive? These are the basic questions underlying the ensuing discussion.

The splendor of Baal emanates from the mountains of the North; the advent of Yahweh emanates from the peaks to the South. Association with mountains is a feature common to any number of ancient Near Eastern deities and hence not especially significant at this point. It is noteworthy, however, that comparable storm metaphors and imagery are employed to describe certain theophanies of Yahweh, even though the character of Yahweh is nowhere defined as that of a phenomenological storm deity. This point is illustrated by the colorful imagery of Judg. 5:4-5:

O Yahweh, when Thou didst go forth from Seir,
When Thou didst stride forth from the land of Edom,
The earth trembled.[36]
Yea, the heavens dripped,[37]
Yea, the clouds dripped water,
The mountains flowed,[38]
Before Yahweh, the One of Sinai,[39]
Before Yahweh, the God of Israel.

This spectacle of Yahweh's awful coming is apparently a description of Yahweh's intervention in that overwhelming storm which flooded the Kishon and drowned the Canaanite army at Tanaach (Judge. 5:19-22).[40] The emphasis again lies upon the specific purpose of the sovereign interference of Yahweh through the resplendent phenomena of the storm. The storm is not effected by Israel nor is its coming necessarily related to any seasonal need for rain. This theophany is spontaneous, an independent act of self-disclosure to meet the particular historical crisis in Israel's life. It is a theophany against specific foes; indeed, "So perish all thine enemies, O Yahweh" exclaims the poet (Judg. 5:31). Hence the storm and the rainfall are the medium and not the essence of this divine revelation. The purpose of Yahweh's theophany is to reveal His nature as a god whose sovereign activity of salvation and election in Israel is readily discernible and ever present, while the character of Baal's appearance is a seasonal and rather impersonal precipitation of moisture for one and all.

It is natural to ask why the description of Yahweh's advent is given in terms of an overwhelming storm spectacle. One answer may be found in the terminology employed by the response of the psalmist in Ps. 68:5, which reads:

> Sing unto God,
> Sing praise to His name!
> Exalt the "Rider of the Clouds,"
> Yahweh is His name!
> Exult before His advent.

Although there are numerous general references to Yahweh's agitation of the elements of the weather and His overpowering presence in the phenomena of the storm and the tempest, the application of this particular epithet, "Rider of the Clouds" to Yahweh the God of Israel, can hardly be accidental. This is the precise title applied to Baal in Canaanite mythology, a title which is used to express a distinctive characteristic of Baal in a culture contemporaneous with that of Israel.[41] This evidence suggests that the relevant passages may reflect a conscious religious polemic against Baal both in the borrowing of Baal's distinctive title as the storm god "who rides the clouds" and in the application of similar storm imagery to the advent of Yahweh from the heavens. The points of similarity in the storm theophany are obvious. Yahweh appears from the mountains accompanied by a profusion of clouds and rain as well as considerable disruptive activity on earth in order to rout those Canaanites (Judg. 5:19) whose god is none other than Baal himself. Yahweh not only deals with Israel's foe but exposes the impotence of the gods of Israel's enemy.

Even the cultic remembrance of Yahweh's self-disclosure in the leading of Israel through the wilderness is described in terms of a storm theophany. One significant portrait is given in Ps. 68:8-10:

> O God, when Thou didst go forth before Thy *people*,
> When Thou didst march through the wilderness,
> The earth trembled,
> Yea the heavens dropped,
> Before God, the One of Sinai,
> Before God, the God of Israel.
> Rain in abundance Thou didst shower abroad, O God,
> As for Thy languishing *heritage*, Thou didst revitalize it.[42]

Once again it is clear that the storm theophany is not an end in in itself, for here, too, the election or redemption motivation is paramount.[43] Yahweh reveals Himself for His *'am,* He appears for the sake of His *naḥạlā* (cf. Deut. 32:9); He acts to save His elect. The storm imagery, on the other hand, stresses that Yahweh and not Baal is the God of all theophany. As the wording of Deut. 33:26 makes clear, there is no god who can compare with Yahweh in splendor; it is He, not Baal who is the "Rider of the Clouds" and the "Rider of the Heavens."[44] The polemical implications cannot be avoided in these lines:

> There is none like God, O Jeshurun,
> Who rides the heavens mightily,
> Who rides the clouds gloriously.[45]

Similar polemical overtones are evident in later passages, such as Hab. 3:3-15, where Yahweh arrives from the mountains of Paran attended by pestilence and plague just as Baal appears accompanied by Reshep the god of pestilence. Yahweh appears with His lightning spear in hand and His chariot of clouds to execute His wrath upon river (Nahar) and sea (Yam), just as Baal, who also brandishes a lightning spear, rode the clouds to victory against Judge Nahar and Prince Yam.[46]

This allusion to pestilence (*rešep*) accompanying the advent of Yahweh in a storm theophany as one of the subservient agents of his activity and subsidiary manifestations of his presence leads to a second major feature of the storm revelations of Yahweh. Rešep is a minor deity attendant upon Baal in Canaanite mythology.[47] Does this fact shed new light upon the appearance of heavenly beings attendant upon Yahweh in certain of the poetic descriptions of His theophanies for Israel? Although II Sam. 22:11 simply speaks of a cherub which was a medium of speedy transportation across the heavens, in Deut. 33:2 the annunciation of Yahweh's coming is depicted as follows:

> Yahweh came from Sinai,
> He dawned upon them from Seir,
> He shone from Mount Paran,
> With Him were myriads of holy ones,[48]
> At His right hand fire came upon them.

"Holy ones" are associated with Yahweh's appearance in this theophany. Elsewhere in the Old Testament, as well as in the Ugaritic texts, the "holy ones" are synonymous with the "sons of gods" (Ps. 89:6-8; Exod. 16-11 according to the Septuagint). There can be little doubt that they are heavenly beings of some kind. It seems logical to argue that in stressing the role of Yahweh as the God of revelation in the theophany, heavenly powers are seen applauding His advent and are all portrayed as willing servants of His supreme will. The theophanic supremacy of Yahweh is the point at issue. It is Yahweh as King and not Baal to whom all heavenly forces and beings pay homage. In other words, the allusions to heavenly beings in such passages are polemically relevant. All such holy ones are but subsidiary personnel in the heavenly assembly, all are worshipers of Yahweh rather than of Baal. Yahweh, unlike Baal, is the sovereign lord who does not need the permission of El for His temple theophany. He comes from His holy ones to conquer the sea (Yam) and destroy Rahab, as the polemic of Psalm 89:6-11 expresses it:

> Let the *heavens* praise Thy wonders, O Yahweh
> Yea Thy faithfulness in the assembly of *the holy ones!*
> For who in the *clouds* is like Yahweh?
> Who is like Yahweh among *the sons of the gods?*
> He is El feared in the council of *the holy ones,*
> Great and terrible above *all who are around Him!*
> O Yahweh, God of hosts,
> Who is as Mighty as thou art, O Yahweh,
> With Thy faithfulness around about Thee?
> Thou dost rule *the sea* with power,

Thou dost still its waves with ruthlessness,
Thou didst *crush Rahab* like a carcass,
Thou didst *scatter* Thine enemies with Thy mighty arm.[49]

In the language of Israelite polemics, Yahweh has usurped the honor of the heavenly powers as well as all the theophanic prerogatives that Baal once exercised, and has controlled with sovereign ease every power that once threatened Baal's kingship. For Yahweh is *El* and hence unrestricted in His self-revelation. Thus the sovereignty of Yahweh is the primary religious thrust in these passages, while the poetic imagery reflects the polemical atmosphere in Israel's conflict with the Canaanite religious culture of that day.[50]

Yahweh's Theophany from His Temple

The integral relationship between the theophany of Baal and his temple is obvious, even though the Canaanite worshiper may not have made a clear distinction between the appearance of Baal from his heavenly temple, as in the Baal myth, and his advent from its earthly counterpart where an attendant sympathetic ritual was probably performed in the presence of some visible replica of his personality. A similar dual perspective seems to be reflected in a number of Old Testament passages where the meaning is elucidated by the presupposition of a heavenly temple as the origin of Yahweh's advent in the storm.

Baal's spectacular self-revelation in the forces of the storm was dependent upon two factors; namely, the erection of a suitable temple (*hkl*) within which to express his essential kingship and a window in the temple as the point of exit from which to appear in regnal splendor. The heavenly temple was both a fitting locality for divine self-disclosure as king of cosmic forces and a suitable point of departure for a theophanic advent.[51] Similar concepts may be present in certain Old Testament passages.

Psalm 11:4, for example, offers an explicit parallelism between "in the temple" and "in the heavens." The text reads:

> Yahweh is in His holy temple (*hēkāl*),
> Yahweh's throne is in heaven.
> His eyes behold,
> His eyelids test the sons of man.

An allusion to a heavenly temple which is at the same time the palace of the king, seems probable. Similarly in Mic. 1:2-4 some such temple is the point of departure for Yahweh's descent in the storm in connection with His advent in judgment:

> Hear, you peoples all of you,
> Hearken, O earth, and all that is in it,
> And let Yahweh be a witness against you,
> Yahweh from His holy temple (*hēkāl*),
> For behold Yahweh is coming forth from *His place* (*māqōm*),
> He will *aescend* and tread on high places of the earth,
> The mountains will melt before Him,
> And the valleys will be cleft.

In the archaic Song of David in II Sam. 22:7-16, the saving intervention of Yahweh on behalf of the entangled worshiper is not only portrayed in the imagery of a brilliant electrical storm, but this divine appearance actually emanates from the temple (*hēkāl* v. 7). Thus just as Baal had done in the well-known Baal myth, "Yahweh thundered forth from heaven, Elyon uttered His voice" (II Sam. 22:14).[52]

The reference to a temple in Psalm 29 is also pertinent.[53] Here the worshipers are heavenly beings whose response to Yahweh's overwhelming self-manifestation in the storm is made from a temple which is logically the heavenly abode of Yahweh. ". . . in the temple (*hēkāl*) all of them cry 'Glory' " is the psalmist's description of this exultant response. So, too, in Psalm 68:34-36 Yahweh, as the "Rider of the Clouds" resides in a heavenly sanctuary (*miqdāš*) amid the clouds. However, even in these cases the Israelite worshiper is, no doubt, located in the earthly sanctuary where the glorious manifestation of Yahweh is also seen in faith, so that the fluctuation of perspective between the heavenly and the earthly presence of Yahweh is understandable. It is not surprising that the earthly shrine of Yahweh was thought to have a heavenly model or archetype as in Exod. 25:40 (Cf. Heb. 9:23f.). Thus, just as in the Baal texts divine kingship and the temple, which is a royal palace, are inseparable, and the presence of this house is essential for divine self-disclosure from the heavens, so, too, Yahweh deigns to have His heavenly kingship depicted in similar culturally relevent terms—His personal revelation expressed in comparable storm terminology, and His kingship linked with a temple as His palace, a temple having both heavenly and earthly dimensions.[54]

Psalm 29: Yahweh's Expression of Divine Kingship in a Storm Theophany

Psalm 29[55] provides a suitable text for a recapitulation of the major points of comparison between the respective storm theophanies of Yahweh and Baal. Thus the initial exordium to acknowledge the character (*šēm*) of Yahweh as King is addressed to those heavenly beings who are associated with Yahweh in this vivid manifestation of His royal supremacy. For it is not Baal but Yahweh who is exalted in the heavenly assembly as the God of revelation.[56] The opening lines read (Ps. 29:1-2):

> Ascribe to Yahweh,
> O heavenly beings,
> Ascribe to Yahweh
> Glory and strength.
> Ascribe to Yahweh,
> The honor of His name,
> Worship Yahweh
> In the revelation of His holiness.[57]

This theophany of holiness is seen in the forces of the storm, in the forceful and exciting voice which issues from the heavenly abode, in great floods and tempestuous winds, in widespread upheavals and disturbances throughout the land, and in the splendor of the lightning flash across the heavens. The same terminology is found elsewhere in the Old Testament and in the Baal text discussed above. Thus it is not the voice of Baal, but the voice of Yahweh, whose thunderous cries of self-expression in nature evoke universal response (Ps. 29:3f.):[58]

> The voice of Yahweh upon the waters,
> The God of glory thunders,
> Yahweh upon many waters,
> The voice of Yahweh with power,
> The voice of Yahweh with splendor.

It is the cataclysmic intervention of Yahweh, and not of Baal, which makes "Lebanon skip like a calf and Sirion like a young buffalo" (Ps. 29:6). Hence it appears that in the use of precisely this storm imagery the Israelite worshiper acknowledges and confesses that it is Yahweh, and not Baal, who is the God of theophany and revelation.[59]

The supremacy of Yahweh over all forces and beings is subsequently acclaimed in the heavenly temple, for at the sound of this resplendent voice "All in His temple cry 'Glory' " (Ps. 29:9). Thus it is not Baal but Yahweh who is the sovereign Lord of the heavenly palace by virtue of His glorious theophany from its windows (as in Gen. 7:11). Yahweh's advent is not dependent upon El's approval, for Yahweh is the El of *kābōd* (Ps. 29:3). Consequently it is not Baal but Yahweh who is enthroned as King above the flood (Ps. 29:10).

The unique feature of this theophany, however, is its personal dimension. The exhortation to magnify the name of Yahweh as well as the vivid portrayal of Yahweh's supreme kingship in the phenomena of nature are but a prelude to the worshiper's plea that the God of revelation exercise this sovereign power on behalf of His *'am* and impart *šālōm* to His elect. Thus the final lines read (Ps. 29:10f.):

> Yahweh sits enthroned above the flood,
> Yahweh sits enthroned as king forever!
> May Yahweh give strength to His people,
> May Yahweh bless His people with peace.

In brief, the portrayal of Yahweh's advent in the storm in no way suggests that Yahweh is a storm god. On the contrary, it underscores that fact that Yahweh, not Baal, is King over all the forces of weather and cosmos, and that in such a theophany Israel can witness the presence of that God who reveals Himself primarily to make a personal choice of people rather than to bless nature. In other words, these theophany passages, especially in this archaic Hebrew poetry, probably express a forceful polemic against Baal as the storm god, and emphasize the distinctive intervention of Yahweh for a particular people as the ultimate purpose of these spectacular appearances. In the conflict between the faith of Israel and the Canaanite religious culture, the storm image was apparently employed to emphasize the truth that Yahweh's involvement in history and life was not obscure or hidden and rarely *suaviter in modo*, but was frequently spectacular or disruptive and always *fortiter in re* beyond anything that the limited kingship of Baal permitted. It served to magnify the *magnalia* of Yahweh and highlight the sovereignty of His choice of Israel in its polemic against Baal worship.

NOTES

[1] The cycle of texts under discussion in this chapter includes primarily Baal V iii 47 - vi 25 and Baal II. Gordon, *Ugaritic Manual*, pp. 188f., 139-44, numbers them Anat III 29 - VI and text 51. The idea of personal theophanies to heroic individuals is also common to Canaanite epic thought. See Aqhat II v-vi; Keret I i-iii; III ii.

[2] Compare Kapelrud, *Baal in the Ras Shamra Texts*, pp. 50-52; W. F. Albright, *Archeology and the Religion of Israel*, p. 75.

[3] C. Schaeffer, *The Cuneiform Texts of Ras Shamra-Ugarit* (London: Oxford University Press, 1936), plate XXXII, figure 2.

[4] Aqhat I i 43f.; Baal I* ii 7; II iii 10, 17; V ii 40.

[5] Baal V iii 41-43.

[6] The term *hmlt* could readily be translated "rain storm" or "flood" which meanings would be quite appropriate in Jer. 11:16 and Ezek. 1:24. The secondary meaning of Arabic *hamala* "rain steadily" or "flow abundantly" would tend to support this suggestion.

[7] Baal I* v 7f.

[8] Baal I* v 10; II i 14, iv 55; V i 23, iii 21. The name Ṭly means something like "Dewy" and 'Arṣy is apparently associated with the earth which Baal must fertilize. It is highly probable that the expression *tal 'ōrōt* in Is. 26:19 is related to these titles.

[9] Baal III B 33.

[10] Baal V i 21-25, iii 26-46. Whether the fertility gods and goddesses invited to Baal's banquet at the completion of the palace in Baal II vi 45-54 are also part of his retinue is not at all apparent from the text.

[11] Baal V ivb 7 - v 9.

[12] Baal II i 1 - ii 29. For a detailed discussion of the furniture mentioned here see W. F. Albright, "The Furniture of El in Canaanite Mythology," *Bulletin of American Schools of Oriental Research*, XCI (1943), 39-44. The structure involved seems to be some form of throne (*kht*) with a canopy and litter borne by two poles overladen with gold.

[13] Baal II iii 9-13. The force of this passage is brought out by T. Gaster, "A King without a Castle," *Bulletin of American Schools of Oriental Research, CI* (1946), 21-34.

[14] Cf. Hebrew *ndd* "retreat." Here the sense is apparently to stand at a distance from the insulted person. The other gods, all of whom possess houses, are the mockers.

[15] The meaning of Ugaritic *qlṣ* is the same as that of Hebrew *qls*, even though there is apparently no direct etymological connection.

[16] Baal II v 6-9. Gray, *The Legacy of Canaan*, pp. 40f., claims that this passage provides the clue to the *Sitz im Leben* of the texts as part of the Canaanite New Year Festival.

[17] Baal II v 20-57. For a fuller discussion of Baal as the builder of the temple see Kapelrud, *Baal in the Ras Shamra Texts*, pp. 110-17.

[18] U. Cassuto, "The Palace of Baal," *Journal of Biblical Literature*, LXI (1942), 51-56. Gray, *The Legacy of Canaan*, p. 42, sees this as a literary device which serves to emphasize a particular feature of the accompanying ritual.

[19] In Baal II vi 10f. Baal himself suggests this explanation by expressing his fear that his daughters Pdry and Tly would leave prematurely and that Yam would laugh at him.

[20] Baal II vii 17-19. Gray, *The Legacy of Canaan*, p. 43, on the basis of an Arabic root (*wdq*) translates the last line, "And let the clouds be opened with rain."

[21] This noun for "window" (*'urbt*) and the verb "to open" (*ptḥ*) are identical with the corresponding terms in the rain sequence of Gen. 7:11.

[22] T. Gaster, *Thespis* (New York: Henry Schuman, 1950), p. 181.

[23] Baal II vi 36-61.

[24] Baal II vii 30-41. See especially the translation of G. R. Driver, *Canaanite Myths and Legends*, p. 101, at this point.

[25] Baal II vii 42-44. G. R. Driver, *ibid*, p. 101, translates the first line "Baal forthwith returns to his mansion." However, the root *yṯb* is frequently used in Ugaritic and Hebrew to designate sitting on a throne. Note especially Ps. 29:10 "Yahweh sits enthroned over the flood."

[26] On this point note also Kapelrud, *Baal in the Ras Shamra Texts*, p. 110.

[27] This is also apparent from the stele of Baal found at Ugarit; see footnote 3 *supra*. Despite the fact that Baal is a young god, and presumably a recent deity in the Canaanite pantheon, the present writer can find no clear evidence that the theophany of Baal reflects a specific historical event which has been mythologized.

[28] The suggestion of C. Schaeffer, *The Cuneiform Texts*, p. 68, that the staircase in one of the towers of the Baal temple is designed to give access to a skylight or window of some kind which was part of the original structure is plausible. If this were true, then the Baal temple at Ugarit would correspond in this detail at least to its heavenly counterpart.

[29] Note especially the sober appraisal of A. de Guglielmo, "Sacrifice in the Ugaritic Texts," 196-216. On the basis of the actual sacrificial terminology, Gray, *The Legacy of Canaan*, p. 146, concludes, "From such sporadic evi-

dence, it is very precarious to assume a sacrificial system such as is found in the 'Mosaic' law."

30 Cf. Guglielmo, "Sacrifice in the Ugaritic Texts," p. 216.

31 Keret I iv 2-8.

32 Gray, *The Legacy of Canaan*, p. 99, translates "serve" and relates the term to the Hebrew root *śrd*.

33 Keret I iv 34-43.

34 It must be emphasized that the reconstruction of Gray, *The Legacy of Canaan*, pp. 147-52, is based upon the analogy of the seasonal cult patterns and the subject matter of the myth itself, not upon details of a ritual which are specified. It is quite possible that certain ritual instructions do accompany the text of Shachar and Shalim. See the interpretation of T. Gaster, "A Canaanite Ritual Drama," 49-76. There is no obvious connection between this text and the Baal myth, however.

35 For the most consistent and complete presentation of the theory concerning the myth-ritual pattern in the ancient world and in primitive thought forms see Gaster, *Thespis*. For the necessary precautions concerning this theory see R. de Langhe, "Myth, Ritual and Kingship in the Ras Shamra Tablets," pp. 132-34.

36 Earthrending disturbances are a frequent characteristic of storm theophanies. Note Baal II vii 30-35. See Ps. 77:19; Hab. 3:6, *et passim*.

37 Note that *šmm* (heaven) seems to be synonymous with "clouds" or "rain" in several Ugaritic passages, e.g., Baal II viii 23; III ii 25; IV i 5; V v 18. Hence the lack of an object presents no difficulty.

38 The translation "flow" suits the context admirably and follows the present vocalization of the Massoretic Text. The Septuagint rendering assumes a root *zll* "to shake," which is also suitable but less likely. Cf. Mic. 1:4, for example, and the parallel passage in Ps. 68:10.

39 The present writer agrees with the position of W. Albright in rendering the text "the One of Sinai" both here and in Ps. 68:9. The grammatical usage is illustrated by the title of El in the Ugaritic texts, to wit, *ṯr 'il d p'id*, "Bull El, the One of Heart." See W. F. Albright, "The Song of Deborah in the Light of Archeology," *Bulletin of the American Schools of Oriental Research*, LXII (1936), 30.

40 While it is true, as A. Weiser maintains, that many cultic expressions are also present in this poem, the context argues against making this theophany simply a theophanic portrait of Yahweh's advent in the cultus as may be the case elsewhere. See A. Weiser, "Das Deborahlied," *Zeitchrift für die alttestamentliche Wissenschaft*, LXXI (1959), 67-97.

41 This Ugaritic parallel is frequently mentioned. Cf. Gordon, *Ugaritic Manual*, p. 200; Albright, "A Catalogue of Early Hebrew Lyric Poems," p. 18, *et alii*. Its full polemic implication, however, needs to be given greater emphasis.

42 Compare the plausible rendering of Albright, "A Catalogue of Early Hebrew Lyric Poems," p. 37. Note the terms *'am*, *naḥạlā*, and the Polel of *knn* which were associated with election in Deut. 32.

43 Compare I Sam. 7:10f.; Josh. 10:10f.; Ps. 77:17-21; Hab. 3:13; II Sam. 22:7-20; Ps. 89:6-11; compare also the storm elements in the theophany at Sinai in Exod. 19:16-19.

44 For the concept of Yahweh riding the clouds, heaven, or heavenly forces, see also Ps. 68:34; II Sam. 22:11f.; Isa. 19:1; Hab. 3:8; Ps. 104:3.

45 See Cross and Freedman, "The Blessing of Moses," 209.

[46] For a detailed discussion of the Canaanitisms in Hab. 3, see W. Albright, "The Psalm of Habakkuk," pp. 1-18.

[47] *Ibid.*, p. 14. Cf. Gray, *The Legacy of Canaan*, p. 96. Compare the association of Reshep with Baal in the Phoenician inscription of Azitawadd from Karatepe. See R. Marcus and I. J. Gelb, "The Phoenician Stele Inscription from Cilicia," *Journal of Near Eastern Studies, VIII* (1949), 115-20.

[48] On this rendering see the vocalization based on the Targum and archaic orthographic usage given by Cross and Freedman, "The Blessing of Moses," p. 198.

[49] The underlined terms indicate, first of all, the relevant parallelism which shows that these beings are heavenly entities present with Yahweh "in the clouds" and second, that Yahweh's victorious coming is described in a manner similar to Baal's conquest of Sea (Yam), by crushing with a mace and scattering abroad. For the role that these verses play in the total context of the Psalm, see J. Ward, "The Literary Form and Liturgical Background of Psalm LXXXIX," *Vetus Testamentum*, XI (1961), 321-39.

[50] For a discussion of these heavenly beings in the wider context, see Wright, *The Old Testament Against Its Environment*, pp. 30-41.

[51] For a treatment of this subject in connection with Exod. 15:17, see Cross and Freedman, "The Song of Miriam," 249f.

[52] Other possible references to the temple in which a heavenly temple could well have been understood include Hab. 2:20; Ps. 18:7 (which is parallel to II Sam. 22:7); Ps. 68:34-36; Jonah 2:7; Isa. 6:1; Pss. 104:3; 150:1.

[53] Cross, "Notes on a Canaanite Psalm in the Old Testament," 19-21, summarizes some of the Canaanite features of the poetic form of the psalm.

[54] Compare the discussion of W. Schmidt, *Königtum Gottes in Ugarit und Israel*, pp. 56-58: Gray, "The Kingship of God in the Prophets and Psalms," 1-29, does not treat this aspect of divine Kingship.

[55] See the treatments by T. Gaster, "Psalm 29," *Jewish Quarterly Review*, XXXVII (1946-47), 55-65, and Cross, "Notes on a Canaanite Psalm in the Old Testament," pp. 19-21, Gaster, *Thespis*, pp. 74-77; A. Johnson, *Sacral Kingship in Ancient Israel* (Cardiff: University of Wales Press, 1955), pp. 54-57; Schmidt, pp. 46-49.

[56] W. Schmidt, *Königtum Gottes in Ugarit und Israel*, p. 47 stresses the fact that El is considered the head of the heavenly assembly in Ugaritic mythology, and that here, "Yahweh das Königtum Els und Baals in sich vereinigte."

[57] The presence of *hdrt* in Keret I iii 51 in the sense of "vision," "theophany" or "divine appearance" argues in favor of the present translation. Cf. Cross, "Notes on a Canaanite Psalm in the Old Testament," p. 21.

[58] The voice of Baal in the sense of thunder is found in Baal II v 8; II vii 29, 31.

[59] The parallelism between Lebanon and Sirion, both locations of Baal's domain from which he obtained cedar for his temple, is apparent in Baal II vi 18f.

Chapter V

BAAL AS THE GOD OF FERTILITY AND YAHWEH AS THE GOD OF LIFE

THE RECHABITES AND NAZIRITES SEEM TO HAVE BEEN part of a broader movement which focused its attention primarily upon the ancient heritage of Israel. "Back to the desert" might well express the party cry of this segment of the community. The unrest of these particular groups, however, was but symptomatic of that tension between Israelite and Canaanite culture which survived for many generations after the initial conflict of the respective early Yahwistic and agricultural ideologies. The compatibility of the religion of Israel with an ancient agricultural way of life was more than an academic question. It is the purpose of this present chapter to accentuate the main features of Baal's role as a god of agriculture and fertility, and to gain a deeper appreciation of the *Spannung* between the early faith of Israel and this aspect of the religion of the Canaanites.

THE DESCENT OF BAAL TO THE UNDERWORLD OF MOT

Encouraged by his glorious self-vindication in the preceding storm theophany, Baal sends an embassy to Mot, the one god who had always claimed his victim in the end. With supreme confidence he dispatches his two lackeys to inform Mot of his triumph.[2] Unfortunately, the details of that message are lost. However, certain features of the character and locale of Mot are clearly distinguishable.[3] While it may be true that Mot is no great favorite of Canaanite worshipers, he is characterized as a son of El, a beloved of El (*ydd 'il*), and a hero (*gzr*) whose dreadfulness is overwhelming. His throne, his house, his domain, and "the land of his heritage" are located in the underworld.[4] Baal's emissary must journey through the huge mountains on the distant horizon where the waters of the underworld reach the surface. Over the realms of the netherworld, it seems, Mot is a king in his own right. In brief, Mot is the god of the underworld. That Baal should claim dominion over this territory was presumptuous indeed.

Mot does not confine his activities to the underworld, however, for any aridity on earth was evidence of his presence at large. Even Shapash (the sun god) may at times humor Mot by concentrating his scorching rays on earth. The relevant passage in Baal II viii 21-24 may be rendered:

nrt 'ilm špš	Even Shapash, luminary of the gods,
ṣḥrrt la' šmm	He burns fiercely [resulting in] no rain,[5]
byd mdd 'ilm mt	By the authority of Mot, darling of El.

Certain passages depict Mot with dragonlike characteristics. Thus the jaws of death can reach, if Mot wishes to extend himself, from the earth below to the heavens above.[6] To die means to be swallowed by Mot himself and literally to enter the bowels of the earth that his appetite might be satisfied.

One thing is clear: Mot is a prominent Canaanite deity whose role is an integral part of the fertility myth which follows. Mot was a reality of nature which each Canaanite had encountered in the fertility drama long before he descended into the underworld himself. In a sense Mot is a fertility god whose presence is needed for ripening the grain and who himself is strewn abroad (and perhaps sown) at the appropriate season.[7] Thus Mot, as well as Baal and Anat, is probably to be included among the major deities involved in this aspect of ancient Canaanite worship.

In the opening lines of tablet I* Mot arrogantly summons Baal to the underworld.[8]

ktmḫṣ ltn btn brh	Though thou didst smite Leviathan the writhing serpent,

tkly bŧn ‘qltn	And didst annihilate the crooked serpent,[9]
šlyṭ dšb‘t r’ašm	The mighty one[10] with seven heads,
tŧkḥ ttrp šmm	The heavens will dry up and languish[11]
krs ’ipdk	Like the dew of thy robe.[12]
’ank ’isp’i	I will consume thee,
’uṭm ḍrqm ’amtm	Thy red blood will be dried up and lifeless.[13]
lyrt bnpš bn ’ilm mt	But now thou must descend the throat of Mot, son of El.

Once the messengers of Baal have relayed the demands of Mot, their hero cannot retaliate. He capitulates without any kind of struggle.[14] Why this sudden reversal of character? Baal had once been renowned as the champion of the gods, the incomparable warrior. The explanation, it seems, lies in the rotation of the seasons. Baal cannot escape the relentless wheel of time. With the advent of summer his lifegiving strength is spent. It needs to be underscored therefore, that the efficacy of Baal as a god of fertility is dependent upon the seasonal cycle of nature itself. Baal is not nature personified but merely one aspect of nature. This reversal of Baal's character is apparent in the text of Baal I* ii 6-12:

yr’a’un ’al’iyn b‘l	Baal the Victor was afraid of him,
ŧt‘nn rkb ‘rpt	The Rider of the Clouds feared him,[15]
. . . .	. . . .
hwt ’al’iy qrdm	The answer of the most valiant of heroes:
bhŧ lbn ’ilm mt	"Hail, Mot, son of El,
‘bdk ’an wd‘lmk	I am your slave, your perpetual slave."

Baal's submission and subsequent descent into the abode of the dead also means the surrender of his personality as the storm god and the god of life-giving water. His entire retinue of lesser moisture gods as well as his "tools of trade"—clouds, wind, rain, and bucket—must accompany him into the rocky graveyard of the netherworld.[16] Thus the death of Baal coincides with the disappearance of precipitation and moisture from the earth. Presumably this is a mythopoetic description of observable natural phenomena. Once Baal has expended himself by the diffusion of his life blood, namely the rain and moisture of the heavens, he permeates the ground as water and descends into the underworld of the earth. With the progress of summer the vitality of Baal gradually diminishes while the forces of aridity increase in order to ripen the grain which Baal has grown. Hence, just as self-disclosure was a fundamental part of Baal's nature as the god of the storm, so here self-expenditure and dying seem to be an essential feature of his nature as a god of fertility.

Baal's function as the god of life and fecundity, however, is not confined to the realm of vegetation. The animal world is also involved. Baal is seen mating with a heifer prior to his descent into Sheol. In the mating season he plants the seed of life to ensure progeny for the forthcoming spring. The relevant passage in Baal I* v 18-22 reads:

yšmʻ 'al'iyn bʻl	Baal the Victor hears,
y'uhb ʻglt bdbr	He loves a heifer in the pasture,[17]
prt bšd šḥlmmt	A cow in the field of šḥlmmt,[18]
škb ʻmnh šbʻ lsbʻm	He lies with her seven and seventy times,
[ ]ly ṯmn lṯmnym	Yea [ ] eight and eighty times,
w [th] rn wtldn mṯ	And she conceives and bears a male.[19]

That some kind of fertility rites accompanied this portion of the myth is quite possible.

Tablet IV which G. R. Driver places at the end of the Baal myth appears to be an elaboration of the mating theme.[20] The tablet in question relates how Anat is found pregnant and gives birth to a bull which proves to be Baal's son. Baal has apparently returned from the underworld at this time. The tablet (Baal IV iii 35-37) concludes with the words:

w'ibr lbʻl [yl] d	Surely a bull is born unto Baal
wr'um lrkb ʻrpt	And a buffalo to the Rider of the Clouds.
yšmḫ 'al'iyn bʻl	Baal the Victor rejoiced.

Apparently Baal's character as the god of life and fertility is dictated not only by man's need for moisture but also by his need for life-giving sperm. Hence Baal takes on the characteristics of the bull, an animal which is basic for Canaanite agricultural prosperity. Here Baal is just as much the deity of sexual life as Anat or Astarte, contrary to what Palestinian archeology seems to suggest. In any case Baal is a god whose sexual activities engender life.

Mortuary Rites for Baal

The death of Baal is portrayed both as a necessity and as a catastrophe. A sympathetic relationship exists between the death of Baal, his followers, and all life. Even El, the head of the pantheon, is appalled at the death of his son when he learns that the inevitable has happened. The passage in question (Baal I* vi 8-10) reads:

lb'l npl l'arṣ	Verily Baal has fallen to the earth,
mt 'al'iyn b'l	Baal the Victor is dead,
ḫlq zbl b'l 'arṣ	Perished is the Prince, Lord of earth.

The details of El's mourning ritual now follow. The way in which the Canaanite worshipers emulated these rites of the gods is not explicit, but the example of their heavenly overlords probably dictated their own actions to a large extent. In the subsequent lines (Baal I* vi 11-16), the role of El, the Father of the gods, involves self-degradation from his throne and self imposed humiliation.

'apnk lṭpn 'il d p'id	Thereupon Lutpan, the compassionate god,
yrd lks'i yŧb lhdm	Descends from the throne, sits on a footstool,
wl. hdm yŧb l'arṣ	Even [descends] from the footstool, sits on the ground.
yṣq 'mr 'un lr'išh	In grief he scatters straw upon his head,[21]
'pr plŧt lqdqdh	In writhing, dust upon his pate.[22]

This agonizing self-torture also includes the rending of garments, vigorous vocal lamentation, and self-mutilation in particular (Baal I* vi 19-20).

lḥm wdqn yŧlŧ	Cheeks and chin he lacerates,[23]
qn ḍr'h yḥrŧ	His upper arm he ploughs;[24]
kgn 'ap lb	His chest like a garden,
k'mq yŧlŧ bmt	His back like a valley he lacerates.

The appellation *dp'id* "the compassionate one," is appropriate for El at this point. This divine pathos of El, this emotional self-expenditure of the father of mankind, is exaggerated by the preceding mortuary rites. The empathetic activities of El reflect the psychological experience of worshipers caught up in a seasonal complex of existence. The spirit of the fertility cult worship, it would seem, is in harmony with the seasonal activities of the gods. Ritual suffering, however, is not vicarious but sympathetic. Frenzied and agonizing lamentation routines form an integral part of the fertility cultus. Such rituals reveal the peculiar seasonal nature of divine compassion or feeling in Canaanite mythology. The pathos of El is free from any moral overtones.

At the end of this tablet, Anat is found searching the countryside for the corpse of Baal. Another tablet (Baal I) relates how Anat performed the same mortuary rites as El and engaged the assistance of Shapash to transport the body of Baal to the mountains of Ṣapon, the traditional abode of Baal. There she wept bitterly for him and honored his burial with a mortuary holocaust of oxen, sheep, deer, goats, and asses. Although the latter may not be sacrifices to the actual person of Baal, they are, nevertheless, offerings in honor of the dead god and apparently a legitimate part of lamentation rites in the fertility cultus.

The nature of the subsequent interregnum is difficult to determine (Baal III i 1-39). The new king chosen to replace Baal is *'ṯtr* (Athtar), an astral deity.[25] His candidacy is supported by Athirat, the queen mother. Whether this interim activity of Athtar reflects some former historical era when an astral cult of alien tribes was making serious inroads into the religious life of Canaan cannot be demonstrated conclusively.[26] In any case, the significance of this god in the fertility cultus of Canaan seems quite secondary here.

The Harvesting of Mot and the Revivification of Baal

"Mot is the god of the corn. He undergoes the fate which overtakes the crops and to which the grain-god is therefore universally subjected." This is the conclusion of Vivian and Isaac Jacobs concerning that portion of tablet three which follows.[27] Quite plausibly Mot, or Death, is also a positive force which expresses itself in heat, drying, ripening, and the like. But the question still remains whether the subsequent winnowing, grinding, and scattering of Mot necessarily implies that he is a grain god in the strict sense, or whether harvesting is but one part of a broader personality. In any case Vivian and Isaac Jacobs have overlooked one major problem, namely, that Baal's title is *bn dgn*, "son of Dagon," or "son of the grain god." In point of fact then if Mot were considered the god of grain (that is Dagon), he would also be the father of Baal, a relationship which is not expressed elsewhere.

The text in question deals with Anat's relentless intercession to Mot for the release of her brother and husband. As the months drag on, the summer heat becomes more intense. Finally, at the time of harvest, Anat's hour has come. With vengeful enthusiasm she reaps Mot who now becomes the bread of life, just as Baal had been the water of life (Baal III ii 30-36):

t'iḫd bn 'ilm mt	She seizes Mot, son of El,
bhrb tbq'nn	With a blade she slashes him,
bḫṯr tdrynn	With a flail she winnows him,
b'išt tšrpnn	With fire she parches him,
brḥm tṭḥnn	With millstones she grinds him,
bšd tdr'nn	In the field she strews him.

The dramatic activity of the goddess Anat in her harvest treatment of Mot immediately suggests that a similar rhythmic ritual activity was performed in the temple cultus itself. The precise nature of this ritual is uncertain. More than likely it involved the offering of first fruits from the harvest or the ritual presentation of the last sheaves prior to public consumption of the sacred new crop.

After the ritual harvesting of Mot, El has a dream which anticipates the revivification of Baal and the restoration of fertility on earth. Once again El ascends the throne, expresses exuberant joy, and implores the aid of Shapash to locate Baal so that the parched furrows of the field may be kissed anew with life-giving rain. The relevant text reads (Baal III iii 10-21):

bḥlm lṭpn 'il dp'id	In a dream of Lutpan, the compassionate god,
bḍrt bny bnwt	In a vision of the creator of created things,
šmm šmn tmṭrn	The heavens rained oil,
nḫlm tlk nbtm	The valleys ran with honey.[28]
šmḫ lṭpn 'il dp'id	Lutpan, the compassionate god, rejoiced,

p'nh lhdm yṯpd	He placed his feet on the footstool,
wyprq lṣb wyṣḥq	He opened wide his gullet and laughed,[29]
yš'u gh wyṣḥ	He raised his voice and shouted:[30]
'aṯbn 'ank w'anḥn	"Now I will sit [enthroned] and rest,[31]
wtnḫ b'irty npš	And my soul shall rest in my breast,[32]
kḥy 'aliyn b'l	For Baal the Victor is alive,
k'iṯ zbl b'l 'arṣ	For the Prince, Lord of earth, exists."[33]

The revival of Baal coincides with the renewal of nature. This renewal is here expressed in terms of the ideal. Honey and oil, the richest commodities of life, are seen flooding the heavens and the earth. The moment of new life dawns with the overwhelming expectancy of perfect *šālōm;* for spring is the glorious *eschaton* of the fertility cultus. The cycle of nature is dependent upon the mood and vitality of the gods and vice versa. The jealousy of the gods is but the passion for survival; the sympathy of nature but a progress report of their endeavors.

The conclusion of the Baal tablet has evoked considerable comment. For after the return of Baal to earth and his summary dismissal of the renegade deities who had usurped his throne, a bitter rivalry exists between Baal and Mot. Mot complains that because of Baal he has been disgraced and humiliated by the constant routine of reaping, winnowing, grinding, and sowing (Baal III v 1-21). This is presumably a reference to the annual harvest cycle. At the end of seven years, Mot, who is also aggravated by Baal's assassination of Mot's half brothers, challenges Baal to a duel (Baal III vi 10-35). The precise outcome of this heavenly encounter is not clear. The so-called Hadad text offers a similar theme in which a drought persists for seven years as a result of an act of fratricide by Baal. But one thing is clear. The descent of Baal into the underworld in the preceding cycle is not the result of a battle against Mot. In that cycle Baal's capitulation was quite docile and apparently a necessary consequence of the seasonal rotation. The final Baal-Mot conflict, then, would appear to be an abnormal rather than a seasonal activity. Presumably it refers to an extended period of drought or to the observance of a sabbatical year.[34] Any further conclusions are impossible because of the fragmentary nature of the texts involved.

It is the conviction of the present writer that the portrait of Baal thus presented is explicable only on the basis that Baal was both a fertility god and a seasonal god, although his role is not necessarily limited to the latter. Many of the activities of the gods are cultic in character and suggest a comparable cultic activity or an accompanying ritual which may or may not be a reenactment of the dramatic incidents of the myth. It is noteworthy that the cycle of Baal's death and revival covers the entire agricultural year. The time of the ritual celebration of this cycle is therefore debatable. The text itself offers no explicit guidelines in the matter. The common inference that all of these events were dramatized at a New Year Festival is a somewhat gratuitous assumption based upon the imperfect analogy of isolated ancient Near Eastern parallels.

Finally, it can be said that the fertility cultus of Canaan apparent from these passages incorporates the roles of Baal, Anat, and Mot. The disposition of El and of nature is dependent upon the fate of these deities. And the sympathetic ritual response of the worshipers may well form an integral part of the fertility cultus.

Drought and the Sympathy of Nature in the Old Testament

From the earliest Israelite literature to the most imaginative apocalyptic nature is considered kerygmatic. For just as the "heavens declare the glory of God," so the locusts proclaim His wrath. There is an integral relationship between the natural order and the moral order. The moral jealousy of Yahweh may express itself by reversing or restoring this cycle of nature. For the sympathy of nature often coincides with the moral and religious activities of the people of God.[35]

In Deut. 32:22-24, for example, the jealous ire of Yahweh, kindled by the idolatrous practices of Israel, is portrayed as a consuming fire that burns off all vegetation, creates famine, leaves pestilence in its wake, and reaches to the very depths of the cosmos. Elsewhere, the same cosmic fire disrupts all natural order to dry up even the fathomless water of the deep and consume the personal land of Israel (Amos 7:4).[36] In Deut. 32:22-24 neither the realm of Mot (Sheol and Tehom) nor the haunts of Baal among the lush pastures are immune from the withering blast of Yahweh's anger. And the subsequent desolation in no way implies the inefficacy or death of Yahweh. On the contrary, it is a forceful testimony to His dynamic presence and an unequivocal attestation to the jealousy of His character. His moral personality cannot tolerate compromise with the fancies of a fertility religion.

Droughts and famines are frequently threatened as acts of divine chastisement and wrath,[37] while certain periods of sterility are specifically designated signs of Yahweh's jealous anger.[38] At the high point of Baal worship under King Ahab the presence of the seven-year drought was especially significant. Drought and famine are a curse of covenant disobedience.[39] The windows of heaven will only be opened when the Israelites are penitent and faithful.[40] The sympathy of nature, the mourning of the land, and the languishing of its inhabitants are natural consequences when man has broken all moral bounds.[41] The normal cycle of life and nature is completely within the control of Yahweh's sovereign might.[42] Yahweh is neither emotionally nor vitally affected by seasonal variations. Any abnormality within this pattern, however, is a witness to His moral and religious jealousy. There is no obvious accommodation to Canaanite imagery here as though Yahweh were engaged in a battle with Mot or mourning like the aged El in the Canaanite pantheon.

That periods of drought and sterility were often considered direct polemics against the so-called fertility gods of Canaan is quite understandable. What is implicit in the terminology of Deut. 32:21-24 becomes explicit in Hos. 2:11-15 where the reversal of the seasons is designed to bring the harlot Israel to her senses and to humiliate the Baal cultus. Likewise in Amos 4:6-8 famine and drought seem to be directed against a similar Baal worship of that period. The emphasis is continually upon Yahweh as the Lord over nature, the dispenser of fertility who is not Himself a part of its relentless cycle. The role of the Israelite was not adjustment to the forces of nature, but to that will of the jealous God who had chosen him.

From the biblical perspective Yahweh is never portrayed as a nature god, or as the nature God, even for the sake of polemic. His moral will and personal character remain unaffected by nature's variations. While it is true that storm imagery is employed to describe His disruptive advent, the same cannot be said of nature in general. Nature, life, and vegetation are considered kerygmatic but not theophanic, "sacramental" but not personified. The drought motif, in particular, accentuates this position.

Agricultural Rituals in Israelite Society

It seems apparent from the preceding discussion that the Baal myth depicts a fertility religion in the strict sense of the term. In this myth the self-expenditure and sexual expression of the divine personality are prominent features. Likewise, mortuary rites and ritual harvesting are an integral part of the cultus of the gods themselves. That certain aspects of this myth are reflected in the Canaanite cultus described at various points in the biblical record seems quite obvious. Cult prostitution is frequently condemned by the prophets and the high places of Baal exposed for what they are.[43] There are mortuary rites for Baal as well as weeping for Tammuz.[44] The marriage imagery of Hosea upholds the love of Yahweh as a holy love, elective and jealous, unaffected by the erotic impulses of the Baal myth. Throughout the Old Testament there is a violent reaction against the cruder aspects of the Baal cultus.[45] The jealousy of Yahweh could not tolerate this kind of crass syncretism. The derision of Elijah on Mount Carmel illustrates the faithful Israelite's attitude toward the mortuary rites for Baal (I Kings 18:27f.):[46]

> And at noon Elijah mocked them saying: "Cry aloud, for he is a god; perhaps he is musing, or has gone aside, or is on a journey, or perhaps he is asleep and must be awakened." And they cried aloud, and cut themselves after their custom, with swords and lances until the blood gushed out upon them.

Yahweh could not be associated with the religious implications of these rituals for He transcended not only nature but also sex and death.[47] Nor was the verdict of Beth-Peor ever modified![48]

While very few scholars suggest that Israel adopted the crass features of the fertility cultus, there are many who tacitly assume that the agricultural festivals are derived *in toto* from the Canaanite fertility cultus.[49] It must be said, at the outset, that such a position cannot be supported or substantiated from the Baal myths outlined above. Those contexts, moreover, which treat the offering of agricultural first fruits reveal a sharp conflict between Israelite and Canaanite religious culture.[50]

The ritual harvesting of Mot reflects the period of reaping, winnowing, grinding into flour, and sowing (Baal III ii 30-36). It would correspond in time to the biblical Feasts of Unleavened Bread and of Weeks. No offering of first fruits is specified in the Baal text, although some such attendant ritual seems likely. John Gray has stressed the connection between this ritual activity of Anat parching and grinding Mot with the cereal offering of first fruits in Lev. 2:14.[51] The passage reads: "If you offer a cereal offering of first fruits to the Lord, you shall offer for the cereal offering of your first fruits crushed new grain from fresh [or green] ears, parched with fire." This would point to the fact that there were at least certain similarities between Israelite and Canaanite agricultural ritual. Nor can the possibility of some borrowing be ruled out. But anything beyond this is mere conjecture.

In the so-called "Ritual Decalogue" of Exod. 34:10-28; the polemic against the Canaanite fertility cultus is quite forceful. The background for these cultic legislations is the breach of covenant brought about by the golden calf festivities which also had certain Baal worship overtones.[52] The persistent jealousy of Yahweh demands that all Israelite festivals be free from any distasteful Canaanite pollutions. Thus the first fruits of the ground must be brought to the altar three times a year just as all first born males must be offered to God or redeemed from Him. The emphasis lies on offering the first of the new produce as a gift to which Yahweh is entitled.[53] Exod. 34:26 concludes, "The first of the first fruits of your ground you shall bring to the altar of the Lord your God," and adds a sharp anti-Canaanite polemic, "You shall not boil a kid in its mother's milk."[54] The implication seems to be that while the offering of first fruits may be found in Canaanite circles also, none of the distinctively Canaanite practices should be tolerated. It is not the burden of the present chapter to discuss the whole gamut of legislations relating to the three major agricultural festivals.[55] Certain characteristics of these festivals, however, need to be underscored at this point.

In the various legislations concerning these agricultural rites there is no obvious hint of any sympathetic acts either dramatic or superstitious. The rituals involved are apparently a response and not a reenactment of some feature of the natural cycle, or an agitation of the divine powers through some fertility "means of grace." The emphasis lies on giving and joyful appreciation, not upon empathy with nature. No man may appear empty handed before Yahweh on such days (Exod. 23:15; Deut. 16:16). This absence of personal kinship with nature is emphasized by the fact that historical incidents are also connected with the celebration of the festival.[56]

The liturgy for the offering of first fruits (Deut. 26:1-15) brings this theological perspective into sharper focus and reveals a strong anti-Canaanite polemic.[57] In the first place the credo (Deut. 26:5-9) accentuates the historical perspective of the ritual. The offering of first fruits is a token of the total divine gift of Canaan; it is not a plea for fertility in the life of the worshiper by virtue of the rite of offering. "And behold, now I bring the first of the fruit of the ground, which Thou, O Lord, has given me" is the immediate response of the worshiper to the credo (Deut. 26:10). The final offering of the tithe of first fruits is accompanied by a confession which embodies a forceful polemic against the Canaanite fertility cultus. The portion to be offered is here designated the "sacred portion" (*haqqōdeš*). In numerous ancient agricultural societies the offering of this portion meant the desacralization of the remainder of the harvest.[58] Here the worshiper testifies that the present portion has not been contaminated by any Canaanite processes of desacralization. The key passage is usually translated "I have not eaten of the tithe while I was mourning, or removed any of it while I was unclean, or offered any of it to the dead. . . ." (Deut. 26:14). This reference to eating part of the tithe in "mourning" only makes sense if this is an allusion to a ritual mourning for the death of some god, presumably Baal. There is no indication that the Israelite would have consumed his holy tithe anywhere other than at the appointed sanctuary.[59] Some forceful impulse or apparent necessity must have moved the Israelite to break the normal practice.

The temptation to assure himself of agricultural prosperity through participation in the Canaanite fertility cultus seems the most logical explanation. If so, then any Israelite association with the mortuary rites of the Baal cultus would cause uncleanness and explain the references to removing the tithe "while unclean."[60] The third feature of this passage makes the anti-Canaanite polemic even more pointed. Inasmuch as there is no strong evidence that Israelites sacrificed to the spirits of their own dead, or if they did there is no explanation as to why a tithe would be used, the offering of the sacred portion of the harvest must refer to something else. The Canaanite myth given above offers two possible explanations. Either there is an allusion to offerings made to Baal upon his death, in which case the text might be rendered, "I have not offered any of it to the dead one (i.e. Baal)"; or there is a reference to the ritual harvesting connected with Mot, in which case the text can be translated "I have not offered any of it to Mot."[61] In view of the fact that the sacrifices offered for Baal were animals and not grain (Baal I), the latter rendering may be preferable. Hence, the testimony of the confessing Israelite is not simply that he has abstained from eating any of the tithe, but that he has made no accommodation to Canaanite fertility practice by using his holy portion for the desacralization of the harvest in mortuary rites for Mot or Baal.

Yahweh as the Lord of Life

When Baal is revived with the new year of life, the world of nature responds with joy. This response, which is in itself a self-expression of Baal's personality, is portrayed in the preternatural terms of heavens raining oil and valleys running with honey.[62] And although this superlative imagery is frequently employed in the Old Testament[63] it is nowhere a symbol of Yahweh *redivivus*, but of the material and physical dimension of Yahweh's blessing of Israel. Thus even the promised land is a "land flowing with milk and honey" (Deut. 26:9); on the eschatological day of bliss the hills will flow with wine (Amos 9:13).

While it is true that an anti-mythical pathos is found in most of the Old Testament portraits of Yahweh's relation to His creation, the poetic imagery of certain passages in the early literature can be more fully appreciated in the light of the Canaanite concept of nature, life, and vegetation. In the first place it is noteworthy that the earth (*'ereṣ*) is the only secondary agent of creation in Gen. 1:1-2:4.[64] The primary agent is the divine word. Here the sovereign will of Yahweh stands in direct antithesis to the advent of vegetation through the rebirth of Baal from the bowels of "mother earth." *'Ereṣ* is but a responsive agent of the Lord of life, not a divine personification. Elsewhere in the Old Testament, powers or forces which are personified or deified in Canaanite fertility myths are relegated to their proper role in nature. The forces mentioned in Gen. 49:25-26 are a case in point. This passage may be translated:

> By El thy father who helps thee,[65]
> By El Shaddai who blesses thee,
> With the blessings of heaven above,
> With the blessings of the deep crouching beneath,
> The blessings of breasts and womb,
> The blessings of thy father and mother,[66]
> The blessings of the eternal mountains,
> The desire of the everlasting hills.

There can be little doubt that certain of the terms employed in this passage had a decidedly religious connotation in Canaanite culture.[67] The very title *El 'ab* immediately reminds one of *'il 'ab 'adm*, "El father of man" in the Ugaritic texts.[68] A possible mythological heritage behind *tẹhōm* has long been emphasized.[69] The *'pq thmtm* "the sources of the two deeps" is the dwelling place of El in Canaanite mythology.[70] The blessings of heaven, as elsewhere, logically corresponds to the rains from the storm whose personification in the god Baal needs no further elaboration. The expression "the blessings of *šādayim wārāḥam*" may also have its origin in Canaanite imagery. In the Ugaritic texts Anat and Athirat are explicitly called the wet nurses of the gods and actually perform this function for the "miracle" child born to Keret.[71] The breasts (*ṯd*) of the goddess are the source of life and blessing. Moreover, *rḥm* appears as a quasi-proper name either for Anat or Athirat in the expression *šd 'ilm šd 'aṯrt wrḥm*, "the divine breasts, the breasts of Athirat and Raḥam."[72] The reading of the Septuagint for the following line then may well reflect an archaic expression which spoke of God as the father and mother of all life. Further, the mountains in Canaanite mythology were the home of the gods, and were consequently the source of all blessing. They were the locale of Baal's palace and the secret places for his creation of lightning and storm.

The parallel passage in Deut. 33:13-16 offers additional terms and expressions which are significant in Canaanite mythology.[73] The significant lines read:

> With the choicest of heaven, from the dew
> And from the deep crouching beneath;
> With the choice produce of the sun,
> With the rich yield of the moon,[74]
> With the finest of the ancient mountains,
> With the best of the eternal hills,
> With the choicest of earth and its fulness
> And the favor of Him who dwells on Sinai.[75]

Ṭāl "dew" appears in Ugaritic as one of the retinue of Baal. Thus in Canaanite imagery this line could be understood as "With the choicest of heaven from Ṭly." Moreover, both *šmš* "sun" and *yrḫ* "moon" appear as gods in Canaanite mythology, while even *'ereṣ* may be included in the train of Baal as the goddess *'Arṣy*.[76] This catalogue of terms which refer to deities or the abode of deities in Canaanite thought can hardly be ignored in a discussion of the origin of the imagery here employed.[77] The distinctive meaning of this symbolism, however, must be determined from the context of the passages cited.

The primary sphere of Yahweh's self-disclosure is that of history. Thus even in the present context, the God who blesses nature is the God of Israel's history, "the Mighty One of Jacob" (Gen. 49:24), "the Rock of Israel" (Gen. 49:24), the "Father" who elects (Gen. 49:25), "the One who dwelt on Sinai" (Deut. 33:16). And this One is Yahweh Himself, who came from Sinai (Deut. 33:2) to become king in the midst of Jeshurun (Deut. 33:5). For as the opening lines of Deut. 33:13 state, it is Yahweh who dispenses blessing upon His land. All those blessings which follow are but gifts from His hand. There is no indication that the sources of these blessings sound any strong mythological overtones any longer. All of these natural resources, from the sun above to the waters of the deep below, from the spectacular storm that rolls out of the distant mountains to the fertility of field and womb, are at the sovereign disposal of Yahweh. From the earliest literature in Israel the portrait is that of Yahweh as a dispenser of fertility and not as a god of fertility,[78] the God who lives to give life and not a god who is but part of the cycle of life and death.[79]

In short, while there are numerous terms and concepts in the early literature which may have had mythological connotations in the fertility cultus of Canaan, the jealousy of Yahweh excluded any designation of Himself as the fertility god or any practice which might suggest this title. Communion with Yahweh could not be established through nature. His distinctive character eliminated the possibility of His self-expenditure in nature or complete revelation through nature.

NOTES

1 Cf. Jer. 35; Num. 6, *et passim*. Compare W. Eichrodt, *Theology of the Old Testament* (Philadelphia: Westminster Press, 1961), I, 303-06, 316f., and R. de Vaux, *Ancient Israel, Its Life and Institutions* (New York: McGraw-Hill Book Co., 1961), pp. 3-15.

2 This is found in the last section of the Baal II tablet (Baal II vii 45-viii 47). The cycle of texts which treat of Baal's descent into the underworld and his subsequent revival includes, in logical sequence, Baal I*; I; III; IV and perhaps Hadad according to the numbering of G. R. Driver *Canaanite Myths and Legends*, pp. 102-21 and 70-73. Gordon, *Ugaritic Manual*, pp. 146-52 and 137-39, numbers these texts 67, 62, 49, 76 and 75.

3 Gray, *The Legacy of Canaan*, p. 137, considers the role of Mot quite negative, serving merely to provide a suitable antagonist for the Baal drama.

4 Baal II viii 1-19.

5 Both Gordon, *Ugaritic Manual*, p. 316, and G. R. Driver, *Canaanite Myths and Legends*, p. 150, appeal to the Arabic *ṣaḥrā'u* "*burning desert*" to support the translation given. The present reading is apparently an intensified form of the stem *ṣḥr*.

6 Cf. Baal I* ii 1ff.

7 Note also the conclusions of Kapelrud, *Baal in the Ras Shamra Texts*,

pp. 126f., and V. and I. Rosensohn Jacobs, "The Myth of Mot and 'Ali'iyan Ba'al" *Harvard Theological Review*, XXXVIII (1945), 77-109.

[8] For separate treatments of this passage see Albright, "Are the Ephod and Teraphim Mentioned in Ugaritic Literature?" 39-43; "Anat and the Dragon," *Bulletin of American Schools of Oriental Research*, LXXXIV (1941), 14-17; H. L. Ginsberg, "Did Anat Fight the Dragon?" *Bulletin of American Schools of Oriental Research*, LXXXIV (1941), 12-14.

[9] The close verbal parallels between these first two lines and Isa. 27:1 have long been recognized. Cf. Isa. 51:9; Ps. 74:12-15; Enoch 60:7ff., Job. 26:1-3.

[10] The Hebrew root *šlṭ* provides an admirable parallel. Gray, *The Legacy of Canaan*, p. 27, translates "the Foul-Fanged" on the basis of an Arabic root.

[11] For the use of Hebrew *škḥ* meaning "dry up" see Pss. 102:5; 137:5; cf. Albright, "Anat and the Dragon," p. 15. *rpy* is cognate with Hebrew *rph* "to droop."

[12] The present translation takes the form *krs* as a preposition plus a noun from the root *rss* "to moisten." Cf. Ezek. 46:14; Cant. 5:2. The translation of G. R. Driver, *Canaanite Myths and Legends*, p. 103, is dependent upon an emendation to *krks* rendering the text "as the belt of thy robe." For the heavens wearing out like a garment see Isa. 51:6; Ps. 102:27.

[13] *'ṭm* corresponds to Hebrew *'tm* "to stop up." The suggestion of Albright that *drq* (*šrq*) is cognate with Accadian *šarqu* "red blood" and Hebrew *šrq* is plausible (cf. Zech. 1:8), but not conclusive.

[14] Note the conclusions of Kapelrud, *Baal in the Ras Shamra Texts*, pp. 117-20.

[15] There is some uncertainty as to the precise meaning of *ṯt'*: Compare the parallelism of Isa. 41:23.

[16] Baal I* v 5-15.

[17] The sexual connotations of *'hb* are common also in the Old Testament. For the noun *dbr* meaning pasture, see Mic. 2:12; Isa. 5:17.

[18] The meaning of *šhlmmt* is still uncertain. Perhaps the meaning "dying pastures" is possible. Cf. the Arabic *sāhilu mamātin* cited by G. R. Driver, *Canaanite Myths and Legends*, p. 107.

[19] Compare the Egyptian *mesu* "son." The name of Moses (*mšh*) is frequently associated with this noun.

[20] G. R. Driver, *Canaanite Myths and Legends*, pp. 114-19.

[21] *yṣq* literally means "pour out." *'mr* is apparently related to Hebrew *'omer* "sheaf" or *'amir* "fallen grain."

[22] Compare Mic. 1:10 "In Beth-le-aphrah roll yourselves in dust."

[23] *Ṯlṯ* is parallel to *ḥrṯ* "plough." The root seems to imply a threefold scoring of the flesh. Inasmuch as agricultural imagery is employed here it is plausible that some sort of plough or hoe with three prongs is the instrument used.

[24] G. R. Driver, *Canaanite Myths and Legends*, p. 144, relates *qn* to Hebrew *qāneh* in Job 31:22 where it is parallel to *šękem* "shoulder."

[25] See J. Gray, "The Desert God Athtar in the Literature and Religion of Canaan," *Journal of Near Eastern Studies*, VIII (1949), 72-83.

[26] Gray, *The Legacy of Canaan*, p. 54. Gaster, *Thespis*, p. 198, suggests that Athtar was relegated to the role of an irrigation deity whose aid was invoked during the dry seasons when Baal was considered dead.

[27] V. and I Rosensohn Jacobs, "The Myth of Mot," p. 79; cf, Kapelrud, *Baal in the Ras Shamra Texts*, p. 126.

[28] Cf. Amos 9:13; Joel 4:18 (Heb.); Ezek. 32:14; Job 20:17.

[29] *lṣb* is apparently related to the Arabic *liṣbu* "narrow passage, strait." Cf. G. R. Driver, *Canaanite Myths and Legends*, p. 159.

[30] Cf. Hebrew *ṣwḥ* in Isa. 42:11.

[31] The context suggests divine enjoyment and the removal of divine anxiety as the major element in the "rest" of the god. The question may well be asked whether or not the "rest" of God after creation (Gen. 2:2) signifies enjoyment of his labors rather than mere cessation from the creative activity.

[32] Cf. Accadian *irtu.*

[33] In line 8 of the same tablet the translation can be rendered "I know that Baal the Victor liveth." Any connection with Job 19:25, however, is ruled out by the context of the latter.

[34] For a discussion of this question see Gray, *The Legacy of Canaan,* p. 63, and Kapelrud, *Baal in the Ras Shamra Texts,* pp. 128f. Gordon, *Ugaritic Literature,* (Rome: Pontifical Biblical Institute, 1949), pp. 3-5, espouses the position that the seven year cycle is the only cycle involved and that Baal is a fertility god but not a seasonal god. See also Kraus, *Gottesdienst in Israel,* pp. 129-32. For a discussion of the Hadad text see J. Gray, "The Hunting of Baal: Fratricide and Atonement in the Mythology of Ras Shamra," *Journal of Near Eastern Studies,* X (1951), 146-55.

[35] Cf. J. L. McKenzie, "God and Nature in the Old Testament," *Catholic Biblical Quarterly,* XIV (1952), 134-36, who speaks of the "sacramental" character of nature.

[36] The reference to drying up the waters of the deep in Amos 7:4, and the biblical and Canaanite cosmology, suggest that burning up the foundations of the mountains means drying up the great waters of the deep in which the mountains were grounded. This passage may reflect a polemic against Baal.

[37] Amos 7:4; 8:11; Isa. 3:1; 5:6, 13f.; Jer. 11:22; Ezek. 6:11f.; *et passim.*

[38] Jer. 14:1-10; II Sam. 21:1; 24:13; I Kings 17:1; 18:17f.

[39] Deut. 11:14-17; 28:15-24; I Kings 8:35-40.

[40] Deut. 28:1-12; Lev. 26:3-5; I Kings 8:35f.

[41] Hos. 4:3; Jer. 4:23-26; 12:4; Isa. 24:4-6; 33:9; and frequently in apocalyptic literature.

[42] Gen. 8:22; Jer. 5:24.

[43] Hos. 4:12-14; Amos 2:7f.; Num. 25:1-9; Deut. 23:18f.; I Kings 14:24; 15:12; 22:46; II Kings 23:7; *et passim.*

[44] Note especially Hos. 7:14; I Kings 13:27f.; Deut. 26:14; Ezek. 8:14; Zech. 12:11, *et passim.* The suggestion that the lamentation over the daughter of Jephthah is the historization of a fertility ritual creates more problems than it solves (Judg. 11:34-40). Cf. Gray, *The Legacy of Canaan,* pp. 53, 149.

[45] See Albright, *Archeology and the Religion of Israel,* p. 94; McKenzie, "God and Nature," pp. 124-30. See also the comparison of Yahweh and Baal in Hosea by G. Ostborn, *Yahweh and Baal* (Lund: C. W. K. Gleerup, 1956).

[46] For a complete treatment of the Baal polemic of Elijah, see H. H. Rowley, "Elijah on Mount Carmel," *Bulletin of the John Rylands Library,* XLIII (1960-61), 190-219. Compare the bodily mutilation of El at the death of Baal in Baal I* vi 11-23.

[47] Wright, *The Old Testament Against Its Environment,* pp. 22-24.

[48] *Supra,* Ch. I, "The Incident at Baal Peor."

[49] For example J. Morgenstern, "The Origin of the Massoth and the Massoth Festival," *The American Journal of Theology,* XXI (1917), 275-93. De Vaux, p. 491, *et passim* is more guarded in his statements. Lev. 23:10 offers one tradition to the effect that certain agricultural feasts were not celebrated prior to the entry into Canaan.

[50] Exod. 34; Deut. 26.

[51] Gray, *The Legacy of Canaan,* pp. 57, 149.

[52] *Supra,* Ch. I, "The Covenant Renewal at Sinai."

[53] See further de Vaux, *Ancient Israel,* pp. 490f.

[54] The basis for assuming a polemic in these words is found in the text of Shachar and Shalim i 13f. which G. R. Driver, *Canaanite Myths and Legends,* p. 121, renders, "Over the fire seven times the sacrificers cook a kid in milk."

[55] The major code legislations concerning these are found in Exod. 23:14-17; 34:18-24; Lev. 23:1-43; Num. 28:16-29:39; Deut. 16:1-17. For treatments of the festivals see de Vaux, *Ancient Israel,* pp. 484-506; E. Auerbach, "Die Feste im Alten Israel," 1-18. It is not the purpose of the present study to investigate the numerous problems seen in the various accounts of the festivals, but merely to point out where the above Canaanite materials contribute to an appreciation of the same.

[56] The Feast of Unleavened Bread commemorates certain incidents in the exodus history (Exod. 12:33-39) while the Passover was an integral part of that historical course of events. The freewill offering of agricultural produce is immediately a reminder that once ". . . you were a slave in Egypt" (Deut. 16:12). Even the Feast of Booths is associated with the temporary habitations of the Israelites in the wilderness wanderings (Lev. 23:42f.).

[57] The archaic character of the creed in Deut. 26:5-9 has been stressed by G. von Rad, "Das Formgeschichliche Problem des Hexateuch," pp. 11-16. The following features in the remainder of the liturgy also suggest an early period when the danger of adopting harmful Canaanite practices and ideas for the ritual of Israel was a living issue.

[58] Cf. Gray, *The Legacy of Canaan,* p. 57.

[59] Cf. Deut. 12:17f.; 14:23.

[60] It is plausible that the root *b'r* actually refers to the burning or parching of the grain as in Canaanite practice and in Lev. 2:14. However, the broader meaning of *b'r* as "remove" in other parts of Deuteronomy may argue against this suggestion.

[61] See Baal I i 10-29; III ii 30-37. The Hebrew consonantal text could just as readily be vocalized *mōt* as *mēt.*

[62] Baal III iii 10-21.

[63] *Supra,* n. 28.

[64] Note the discussion of G. von Rad, *Genesis* (Philadelphia: Westminster Press, 1961), p. 53. He concludes, "One is reminded unmistakably of the term *natura;* the term, however, is bounded by the term *creatura.*"

[65] Cf. Deut. 32:6,18; Pss. 89:27; 68:6.

[66] The present rendering follows the Septuagint and Samaritan Pentateuch. The Massoretic text may well be a case of dittography, *gbr 'l* being written for *gb't 'lm* of the next line.

[67] For a study of the Canaanite background of the entire chapter see B. Vawter, "The Canaanite Background of Genesis 49," 1-18.

[68] Keret I i 37, 43 *et passim.*

[69] Vawter, "The Canaanite Background of Genesis 49," p. 14.

[70] Baal II iv 22; III i 6. See further, H. L. Ginsberg, "A Ugaritic Parallel to II Sam. 1:21," *Journal of Biblical Literature, LVII* (1938), 209-13.

[71] Keret III ii 25-28; Shachar and Shalim i 24; ii 25, 27.

[72] Shachar and Shalim i 13, 24, 28.

[73] For Deut. 33 in general see Cross and Freedman, "The Blessing of Moses," 191-210.

[74] The parallelism with *šmš* "sun" suggests that *yrḥm* be vocalized as "moon" plus enclitic mem.

[75] The archaic orthography of *snh* would appear as *sn*. The vocalization *sīnē* "Sinai" is therefore plausible. Cf. Samaritan Pentateuch and Judge. 5:5.

[76] *Šmš* appears in Ugaritic as *špš* in Baal III ii 24; III iii 24, *et passim*. The text Nikkal and the Kathirat relates the marriage of Yarikh to Nikkal. *'Arṣy* appears in the retinue of Baal in Baal II i 16; II iv 57.

[77] Vawter "The Canaanite Background of Genesis 49," p. 13, cites an ancient incantation from upper Syria which corresponds in form to the blessing of Gen. 49:25f. Here, just as in the ancient treaties, the heavens, the earth, and various personified powers of nature are considered powers capable of blessing or cursing.

[78] See also Gen. 27:28; Deut. 7:12-15; Pss. 65:10-14; 85:13 and frequently in later literature. The advent of Yahweh and the revival of Baal are hardly comparable incidents as T. Worden seems to imply in his allusions to Pss. 65:10-16; 96:11-13; 104:30; 147:8. T. Worden, "The Literary Influence of the Ugaritic Fertility Myth on the Old Testament," *Vetus Testamentum*, III (1953), 295f. Cf. McKenzie, "God and Nature," p. 126.

[79] In this connection, then, the epithet *'el ḥay* is specially appropriate. While there is no good reason to assume that the concept of Yahweh as the "living God" originated as a reaction against the cult of the dying and rising god, its association with the jealousy of Yahweh is totally relevant at this point.

GENERAL CONCLUSIONS

(a) THE BIBLICAL RECORD ATTESTS TO A CLOSE PREMONarchic contact between the faith of Israel and alien religious cultures.[1] This is confirmed by the conflict traditions concerning Sinai, Beth-Peor, and Shechem among others. The existence of this clash of cultures and, in particular, the Israelite *damnamus* pronounced upon many of the religious beliefs and practices of alien cultures, as well as the tacit *laudamus* to be heard in the Israelite adoption of less offensive religious modes of expression, presupposes the presence of a mutually intelligible circle of religious concepts. And this but serves to emphasize that the life, language, literature, and background of Israel were conditioned by its cultural environment. In the religious milieu of the ancient Near East, Israel was indeed *qādōš* (set apart) but not *nikrāt* (cut off).

(b) The pangs of controversy and conflict have played a significant part in the birth of numerous religious documents. And, as the previous study has shown, the earliest covenant formulations of Scripture are no exception. The specific conflict in these passages, however, is not primarily between factions of Israel, but between Israel and contemporary religious movements of kindred pagan cultures. A knowledge of these religious tensions leads to a deeper understanding of the relevant character of the covenant pericopes, as well as the religious antitheses which they inevitably pose.

(c) In the consequent delineation of Israel's covenant faith three fundamentals were emphasized. Briefly, each Israelite who had witnessed the abnormal intervention of Yahweh in the exodus event and had confronted Him in the covenant moment was thereby moved to acknowledge the *magnalia* of Yahweh, the jealousy of His overlordship, and His sovereign choice of Israel as the *sine qua non* of his own faith and the basis for his covenant communion with Yahweh. The pertinent features of these religious postulates were outlined in connection with the covenant pericope of Exod. 19:3-8 and further illustrated by certain features of the golden calf story, the incident at Beth-Peor, and the Diet at Shechem. In Chapter Two it was demonstrated how the same essentials of the covenant could be traced through the early poetic literature of Scripture.

(d) It was the burden of the subsequent chapters to indicate the specific value and relevance of comparing similar terminology, imagery, and practices found in both Israelite and Canaanite religious culture. In so doing it became evident, first of all, that the fundamentals of the covenant faith are brought into sharper focus. Thus in Chapter Three the *magnalia* of Yahweh's saving activity are seen from the broader perspective of Yahweh's kingship. In Chapter Four the sovereignty of Yahweh is emphasized through His theophanic self-revelation to Israel, while in Chapter Five the avid jealousy of Yahweh is magnified by His activity in nature and His attitude toward agricultural rites.

(e) While certain Canaanite religious concepts and imagery may have been consciously incorporated into early biblical writings, the attitude taken toward other Canaanite beliefs and practices reveals that these were vigorously excluded. In this connection the first significant feature presented was the sequence of religious activities and concepts which are employed to portray the kingship of Baal. A similar pattern of thought was shown to underlie the account of Exod. 15:1-18. The existence of such a pattern in this passage, or elsewhere, does not necessarily imply the adoption of all the religious ideas reflected in the Canaanite original nor the attendant ritual which may have accompanied the recital of this text. Despite the similarity of thought sequence, the religious presuppositions must be first ascertained. In this case, the presuppositions of the respective texts concerning the nature of kinghip are radically different. For the early Israelite the *principium cognoscendi*, that is the normative source of knowledge for his faith, is the message of Yahweh's activity in history, for the Canaanite it is the complex of the cosmos.

(f) The pattern in question, however, does indicate that the kingship of Yahweh is here portrayed in a way which is culturally relevant for the Israelite of that day. It accentuates the archaic character of the kingship of Yahweh concept. This concept is also presupposed by the covenant itself. In brief, the presence of a pattern of religious thought does not necessarily imply that the biblical usage of such a pattern corresponds in every detail, whether theological or cultic, with its mythological counterpart. The *tertium comparationis* must first be established.

(g) It was also shown that comparable religious imagery is common to both Canaanite and biblical literature. Many of these concepts and images, however, can be regarded as a part of the cultural milieu of the Israelite world and do not necessarily presuppose a conscious exchange of ideas. Such imagery may be relevant for an understanding of the *Weltanschauung* of the premonarchic period, but it does not automatically presuppose an identical meaning in all its usages. The religious perspective of the respective cultures must always remain a conditioning factor in any interpretation of such imagery. The previous analysis of Yahweh's advent in the tempest and of Baal's theophany in the storm, as well as of their respective retinues of heavenly beings, was concerned with this question. The concept of the sympathy of nature and the image of Yahweh as a warrior God fall into the same category.

(h) On the other hand, considerable evidence was adduced to suggest that certain imagery and terminology may have been consciously and deliberately adopted by biblical authors in order to express a direct polemic against certain gods or beliefs of the Canaanite religion. This evidence was seen especially in connection with the various antitheses between Yahweh and Baal as the storm god. The portrait of Yahweh in Psalm 29 offers a striking illustration of this point.

(i) While it is apparent that many of the preceding biblical concepts and images can be more fully appreciated by comparison with their Canaanite counterparts, it is also true that identical terms and idioms appear in the respective literatures. The meaning of this terminology, however, may or may not be identical in both cultures. Just as biblical usage and contextual relevance rather than etymology is finally determinitive for the textual meaning of a biblical term, so too the *analogia fidei* found in the essentials of the covenant is pertinent for the complete understanding of the religious or theological meaning of a word in its cultural environment. In other words, a term in Canaanite literature may appear linguistically synonymous with a biblical expressiọn, but bear a totally different or at least significantly modified theological import from its scriptural counterpart. This was demonstrated by the treatment of such terms as *yam*, *hēkāl*, Leviathan, or Mot and by the discussion of the terminology of fertility worship.

(j) It became clear that the biblical record concerning a number of religious practices suggests a direct polemic against certain features of the Canaanite cultus. It was also seen that none of the Ugaritic materials gave any explicit detailed information concerning the origin of Israelite cultic practices. In a few instances, however, pertinent objections to known usages of the Canaanite cultus seem either explicit or implicit. The preceding discussion of the agricultural rites and temple cultus of Baal suggested this as a possible conclusion.

In brief, it has been shown that a conflict of religious cultures is reflected in the biblical record and that the Ugaritic texts are relevant for an appreciation of the conflict between Israelite and Canaanite religious culture in particular. Moreover, it has been demonstrated that these texts are relevant for a deeper understanding of the essentials of Israel's covenant faith, and that valuable insights into the meaning of contemporary biblical materials can be gained by a comparison with similar religious patterns, imagery, concepts, terminology, and practices of the religious culture of Canaan. Perhaps the words of Robert Browning are apt at this point:

> It is by no breath,
> Turn of eye, wave of hand,
> That salvation joins issue with death.
> Saul XVIII: 18f.

NOTE

[1] It is noteworthy that each of the major assertions of the foregoing presentation can be correlated with the text of I Sam. 12:1-15 which is one of the first major documents of the early monarchic period. See Chapter VII of the writer's "Conflict of Religious Cultures."

SELECTED BIBLIOGRAPHY

Aistleitner, J. 'Die Anat-Texte aus Ras Shamra," *Zeitschrift für die alttestamentliche Wissenschaft*, LXVII (1939), 193-211.

Albright, W. F. "Anath and the Dragon," *Bulletin of American Schools of Oriental Research*, LXXXIV (1941), 14-17.

———. *Archaeology and the Religion of Israel.* Baltimore: The Johns Hopkins Press, 1953.

———. "A Catalogue of Early Hebrew Lyric Poems (Psalm 68)," *Hebrew Union College Annual*, XXIII (1950-51), 1-39.

———. "The Oracles of Balaam," *Journal of Biblical Literature*, LXIII (1944), 207-33.

———. "The Psalm of Habakkuk," *Studies in Old Testament Prophecy*. Edinburgh: T. & T. Clark, 1950, pp. 1-18.

———. "Some Remarks on the Song of Moses in Deuteronomy XXXII," *Vetus Testamentum*, IX (1959), 339-46.

Cross, F. M., and D. N. Freedman. "The Blessing of Moses," *Journal of Biblical Literature*, LXVII (1948), 191-210.

———. "The Song of Miriam," *Journal of Near Eastern Studies*, XIV (1955), 237-50.

Cross, F. M. "Notes on a Canaanite Psalm in the Old Testament," *Bulletin of American Schools of Oriental Research*, CXVII (1950), 19-21.

Dahood, M. "The Divine Name 'Eli in the Psalms," *Theological Studies*, XIV (1953), 452-57.

Driver, G. R. *Canaanite Myths and Legends*. Edinburgh: T. & T. Clark, 1956.

Eissfeldt, O. "Baal Zephon, Zeus Casios, und der Durchzug der Israeliten durchs Rote Meer," *Beitrage zur Religionsgeschichte des Altertums*, I (1932).

———. "Das Lied Moses Deuteronomium 32:1-43 und das Lehrgedicht Asaphs Psalm 78 samt einer Analyse der Umgebung des Moses-liedes." Vol. CIV, No. 5 in *Berichte Uber die Verhandlungen der Sächsischen Akademie der Wissenschaften zu Leipzig* (1958).

Freedman, D. N. "Archaic Forms in Early Hebrew Poetry," *Zeitschrift für alttestamentliche Wissenschaft*, LXXII (1960), 101-06.

Gaster, T. H. "A Canaanite Ritual Drama," *Journal of American Oriental Society*, LXVI (1946), 51-76.

———. "A King without a Castle," *Bulletin of American Schools of Oriental Research*, CI (1946), 21-30.

———. "Psalm 29," *Jewish Quarterly Review*, XXXVII (1946-47), 55-65.

———. *Thespis*. New York: Henry Schuman, 1950.

Ginsberg, H. L. "Did Anath Fight the Dragon?" *Bulletin of American Schools of Oriental Research*, LXXXIV (1941), 12-14.

———. "Ugaritic Myths," *Ancient Near Eastern Texts Relating to the Old Testament*. Edited by J. Pritchard. Princeton University Press, 1955, pp. 129-55.

———. "A Ugaritic Parallel to II Samuel 1:21," *Journal of Biblical Literature*, LVII (1938), 209-13.

Gordon, C. *Ugaritic Manual*. Rome: The Pontifical Biblical Institute, 1955.

———. *Ugaritic Literature*. Rome: The Pontifical Biblical Institute, 1949.

Gray, J. "Canaanite Kingship in Theory and Practice," *Vetus Testamentum*, II (1952), 193-220.

———. "The Kingship of God in the Prophets and Psalms," *Vetus Testamentum*, XI (1961), 1-29.

———. *The Legacy of Canaan*. Leiden: E. J. Brill, 1957.

Guglielmo, A. de. "Sacrifice in the Ugaritic Texts," *Catholic Biblical Quarterly*, XVII (1955), 196-216.

Jacob, E. *Ras Shamra et l'ancien Testament*. Neuchatel: Delachaux & Niestle, 1960.

Jacobs, V, and I. Jacobs. "The Myth of Mot and 'Al'iyan Ba'al," *Harvard Theological Review*, XXXVIII (1945), 77-109.

Kapelrud, A. S. *Baal in the Ras Shamra Texts*. Copenhagen: G. E. C. Cad, 1952.

Langhe, R. de. "Myth, Ritual and Kingship in the Ras Shamra Tablets," *Myth, Ritual and Kingship*. Edited by S. H. Hooke. Oxford: Clarendon Press, 1958.

May, H. G. "Some Cosmic Connotations of *Mayim Rabbim*, 'Many Waters,'" *Journal of Biblical Literature*, LXXIV (1955), 9-21.

Mendenhall, G. E. *Law and Covenant in Israel and the Ancient Near East*. Pittsburgh: The Biblical Colloquium, 1955.

Muilenburg, J. "The Form and Structure of the Covenantal Formulations," *Vetus Testamentum*, IX (1959), 347-65.

Obermann, J. "How Baal Destroyed a Rival," *Journal of the American Oriental Society*, LXVII (1947), 195-208.

———. *Ugaritic Mythology*. New Haven: Yale University Press, 1948.

Pope, M. *El in the Ugaritic Texts*. Leiden: E. J. Brill, 1955.

Pritchard, J. *Ancient Near Eastern Texts Relating to the Old Testament.* Princeton: Princeton University Press, 1955.

Schaeffer, C. *The Cuneiform Texts of Ras Shamra-Ugarit.* London: Oxford University Press, 1936.

Schmidt, H. "Das Meerlied," *Zeitschrift für die alttestamentliche Wissenschaft*, XL (1931), 59-66.

Schmidt, W. *Königtum Gottes in Ugarit und Israel.* Berlin: A. Topelmann, 1961.

Vawter, B. "The Canaanite Background of Genesis 49," *Catholic Biblical Quarterly*, XVII (1955), 1-18.

Vida, G. L. D. "El 'Elyon in Genesis 14:8-20," *Journal of Biblical Literature*, LXIII (1944), 1-9.

Worden, T. "The Literary Influence of the Ugaritic Fertility Myth on the Old Testament," *Vetus Testamentum*, III (1953), 273-97.

Wright, G. E. *The Old Testament Against its Environment.* London: SCM Press, 1950.

INDEX TO BIBLICAL REFERENCES

Reference	*Page*
GENESIS	
1:1-2:4	107
2:2	111
2:6	70
4:1	49
7:11	87, 89
8:22	111
14:16	44
14:18-20	48
14:19	42
15:7	32
17:10	28
26:8	34
27:28	113
31:44	33
31:48-52	32
33:9	27
33:20	36, 49
34:1-35:4	28
34:2	27
34:13-17	28
35:1-4	37
49	47, 112, 113
49:2-17	39
49:14	36
49:24	48, 108
49:25	48, 108
49:25f.	113
49:25-26	107
EXODUS	
3:13ff.	15
6:2ff.	15, 49
7:3	31
7:4	31
9:14	33
9:16	33
9:29	33
10:22-26	32
11:9-10	31
12:12	14, 31
12:21-28	14
12:33-39	112
12:36	14
12:38	28, 37
14:2ff.	20
14:4	14, 33
14:18	33
14:28	14
14:30f.	14
15	49, 66, 70
15:1	40, 59
15:1-18	12, 39, 58, 66, 116
15:3	41, 59
15:4-5	59
15:6	40, 60

Reference	*Page*
15:6-8	40
15:7	60
15:9	59
15:10	40, 60
15:11	40, 41, 46, 60, 64, 70
15:13	40, 43, 44, 45, 61
15:15f.	45
15:16	40, 43, 44, 49, 61
15:17	49, 61, 91
15:18	48, 62, 68
15:24	31
15:25	15
15:26	15, 33
16:2	31
16:3	15
16:6	32
16:7	15, 31
16:8	31
16:9	31
16:11	83
16:12	31
17:3	31
17:7	15
18:1	32
18:10f.	33
18:11	15
19:3-6	16, 24, 26, 42
19:3-8	11, 28, 116
19:4	17, 26, 70
19:5	18, 26, 33
19:6	19
19:8	18
19:16-19	90
20:2	32
20:3-5	16
20:4	22, 35
20:5	16, 35
20:22	32
22:17	32
22:19	32
22:20	32
22:21	32
22:27-30	32
23:1-19	32
23:14-17	112
23:14-19	35
23:15	105
23:19	35
23:23f.	15
23:27	49
24:4	32
24:5-11	18
24:7	18
24:13	70
25:40	85
31:18	22

Reference	*Page*
32	34, 35
32:4	21, 35
32:5	21
32:6	22
32:7-14	22
32:8	22
32:10	21
32:19	22
32:30-33	21
32:32	33
33:17-23	22
34	23, 112
34:1-4	23
34:1-28	23, 34
34:6f.	22
34:10	24, 35
34:10-28	104
34:11-13	34
34:11-26	23
34:14	24, 35
34:15-16	34
34:17	23, 35
34:18-24	112
34:26	23, 104
34:28	23
LEVITICUS	
2:14	104, 112
11:45	32
23:1-43	112
23:10	112
23:42f.	112
24:10	37
26:3-5	111
26:13	32
26:45	32
NUMBERS	
3:13	32
6	109
10:29-32	37
10:35	70
12:1	37
14:2	31
14:27	31
14:29	31
14:36	31
16:11	31
16:41	31
17:5	31
22:41	25
23:8	48
23:8f.	43
23:9	48
23:21	48
23:21f.	63

Reference	*Page*
NUMBERS (*cont'd*)	
23:21-23	40, 43
23:22	48
23:23	43, 61
24:4	48
24:9	45
24:16	48
25:1	25
25:1-5	35
25:1-9	111
25:3	24
25:6-9	24
26:1-4	36
28:16-29:39	112
32:38	36
33:50ff.	36
DEUTERONOMY	
1-3	26
1:1	36
1:4	35
1:5	36
1:31	32
3:21	32
3:29	25
4	26
4:1	26, 33
4:1-2	26
4:3	35
4:3f.	26
4:9-14	26
4:15-24	26
4:19	36
4:20	26, 32, 49
4:24	35
4:25f.	26
4:26	25, 32
4:32-39	26
4:34	31, 32
4:39	33
5:1-21	26
5:2f.	36
5:22-33	36
6:8	68
6:12	32
6:20-25	36
6:21	32
7:6	33
7:6-8	33
7:7	32
7:12-15	113
7:17-19	32
7:17-26	36
7:19	32
8:19	33
9:1	36
9:5	33
9:6-21	22
9:26	49
9:29	49
10:12	33
10:21	32
11:2	32
11:7	32
11:13f.	33
11:14-17	111
11:18	68
11:22	33
11:26	36
12:17f.	112
14:2	33
14:21	33, 35
14:23	112
15:5	33
16:1-17	112
16:12	112
16:16	105

Reference	*Page*
20:10-18	36
23:17f.	35
23:18f.	111
26	112
26:1-15	105
26:5-9	105, 112
26:5-10	36
26:9	106
26:10	105
26:14	105, 111
26:16-19	36
26:18f.	33
26:19	33
27:9f.	36
28:1	33
28:1-12	111
28:9	33
28:15-24	111
28:46	31
29:1	32, 36
29:2	32
30:15-20	36
31:1	36
31:9-11	35
32	47, 90
32:1-43	47
32:2	70
32:2-43	39, 47
32:3	48
32:4	41, 48, 68
32:6	43, 44, 49, 112
32:7-14	42
32:8	70
32:8f.	42, 67
32:9	42, 82
32:9f.	42
32:10	43
32:10-12	40, 43
32:12	48
32:15	46, 48
32:15-38	46
32:17	46
32:18	43, 46, 48, 112
32:21	46
32:21-24	102
32:22-24	101
32:23f.	40
32:25	49
32:27	45
32:30	48
32:31	48
32:35f.	45
32:41	40
33	113
33:1	70
33:2	14, 40, 45, 68, 83, 108
33:2-5	43
33:2-29	39
33:3-5	45
33:4	45
33:5	41, 48, 63, 108
33:12	48
33:13	108
33:13-16	108
33:16	108
33:26	41, 46, 82
33:29	40, 41, 43, 45, 48
JOSHUA	
2:9	49
3:11	33
3:13	33
8:24-28	36
8:30	36
9	34
9:14	37
10:10f.	90

Reference	*Page*
11:6-9	27
11:12	36
11:17	36
11:20	36
12:7	36
13:17	36
14:14f.	37
15:10	36
19:27	36
19:38	36
22:17	25
22:34	32
23:3	32
23:12f.	33
24	28, 37
24:2	28, 29, 36, 49
24:2-13	29, 36
24:3	29
24:5	29
24:6	29
24:7	28, 32
24:8	29
24:10	29
24:11	29
24:12	29
24:14	33
24:14f.	29
24:14-18	29
24:15	29
24:16	30
24:19	30, 35, 45
24:22	17, 30
24:23	28, 33, 36, 49
24:24	30
24:25	30
24:27	30, 32
JUDGES	
1:16	37
2:11	36
2:12	32
2:13	36
3:7	36
3:31	36
5:2-31	39
5:3	46
5:4	45
5:4f.	40
5:4-5	80
5:5	13, 40, 44, 45, 70, 113
5:8	45
5:11	44
5:13	44
5:15-17	45
5:19	81
5:19-22	80
5:20	40
5:21	40
5:23	45
5:31	41, 81
6:8-10	32
6:13	32
6:28-32	36
8:23	70
8:33	36
9:7	32
9:28	27
9:46	28
10:6	36
10:10	36
11:34-40	111
20:33	36
I SAMUEL	
2:10	48
4:4	34, 70
7:10f.	90

Reference *Page*
I SAMUEL (*cont'd*)
8:7 70
12:1-15 118
12:7 33
12:12 70
12:13 33
12:14 33
12:25 33
20:12 32
20:23 32
20:42 32
27:10 37

II SAMUEL
1:21 113
21:1 111
22:2 48
22:2-51 39
22:3 48
22:7 91
22:7-16 85
22:7-20 90
22:11 34, 83
22:11f. 90
22:14 48, 85
22:32ff. 48
22:47-49 48
24:13 111

I KINGS
7:36 34
8:2ff. 35
8:35f. 111
8:35-40 111
12:1 36
12:28 20, 21, 29
13:27f. 111
14:24 111
15:12 111
17:1 111
18:17f. 111
18:27f. 103
19:8 70
22:46 111
23 35

II KINGS
23:7 111

II CHRONICLES
14:1-5 35
29:10ff. 35
31:1-3 35
34:31-33 35

NEHEMIAH
8:13ff. 35

JOB
9:13 70
19:25 111
20:17 111
25:12 71
26:1-3 110
26:12 70
31:15 49
31:22 110

PSALMS
7:18 48
8:4 49
11:4 84
18:7 91
18:11 34
24:1f. 66
24:2 49
24:9 70

Reference *Page*
29 40, 85, 86, 91, 117
29:1 70
29:1f. 46
29:1-2 86
29:1-11 39
29:3 87
29:3f. 86
29:6 76, 87
29:9 87
29:10 48, 87, 89
29:10f. 87
33:12 49
42:8 70
46:2f. 66
47 70
48:3 31
50:2 68
54:7 68
57:3 48
65:10-14 113
65:10-16 113
68:1-35 39
68:5 81
68:6 112
68:8-10 82
68:9 90
68:10 49, 90
68:22f. 70
68:25 70
68:28 69
68:34 90
68:34-36 85, 91
69:2f. 70
69:16f. 70
73:27 68
74:12-14 65
74:12-15 71, 110
77:14 68
77:17-21 90
77:19 90
78 47
79:7 70
80:2 68
81:6 32
81:11 32
83:19 42
85:13 113
87:4 70
87:5f. 49
89 91
89:6-8 70, 83
89:6-11 83, 90
89:7 70
89:9f. 71
89:11 70
89:26 70
89:27 112
91:1f. 48
93:1-4 66
94:1 68
94:23 68
95 70
95:5 66
96:11-13 113
99 70
102:5 110
102:27 110
104:3 74, 90, 91
104:5-9 66
104:30 113
106:5 49
106:28 25, 36
124:4f. 70
135:4 33
137:5 110
138:4f. 68
139:13 49

Reference *Page*
143:12 68
144:7 70
145:13 68
147:8 113
150:1 91

PROVERBS
8:22 49
31:3 68

ECCLESIASTES
10:18 68

CANTICLES
5:2 110

ISAIAH
3:1 111
5:6 111
5:13f. 111
5:17 110
6:1 91
9:1ff. 32
14:9 70
14:13 31
19:1 90
24:4-6 111
26:19 88
27:1 110
29:4 70
30:7 70
31:5 31
32:18 70
33:9 111
33:20 70
41:23 110
42:11 111
43:1-7 19
43:8-13 32
43:15-17 71
45:18 49
51:6 110
51:9 110
51:9-11 65
59:18 48
63:7 48

JEREMIAH
2:7 70
4:23-26 111
5:24 111
7:5 33
9:20 76
10:25 70
11:4 32
11:16 67, 88
11:22 111
12:4 111
12:8f. 70
12:16 33
14:1-10 111
16:18 70
22:4 33
31:23 70
35 109
46:1ff. 32
50:7 70
50:11 70

EZEKIEL
1:4 31
1:24 67, 88
6:11f. 111
8:14 111
28:14 31
28:17 68
29:1-5 54

Reference	Page
EZEKIEL (*cont'd*)	
29:1-8	65
29:3-5	65
30:1ff.	32
32:2-8	54
32:14	111
46:14	110
DANIEL	
3:33	68
4:31	68
HOSEA	
1:2	35
2:1-13	35
2:11-15	102
4:3	111
4:11-14	35
4:12-14	111
5:2	25
7:14	111
7:16	48
9:10	25
10:5	48
10:11	68
11:8	48
JOEL	
3:18	35
4:18	111
AMOS	
2:7f.	111
4:6-8	102
7:4	101, 111
8:11	111
9:13	106, 111
JONAH	
2:7	70, 91
MICAH	
1:2	32
1:2-4	85
1:4	90
1:10	110
2:12	110
6:1	32
6:5	35
HABAKKUK	
2:20	91
3	71, 91
3:2-19	39
3:3	14
3:3-15	82
3:5	36
3:6	90
3:8	90
3:13	90
ZEPHANIAH	
3:8	32
ZECHARIAH	
1:8	110
6:15	33
12:11	111
13:6	68
14:5	70
14:19	32
MALACHI	
3:17	33
HEBREWS	
9:23f.	85
ENOCH	
60:7ff.	110

INDEX OF SUBJECTS AND NAMES

Aaron, 21-22, 34 n.28
Abraham, 32 n.16
Agricultural rituals, 103-6
Amphictyony, 27-30, 31 n.1, 35 n.43, 36 n.64
Anath, 18, 27, 48 n.11, 49 n.22, 55-57, 63, 65, 74, 76, 78, 94, 96, 98, 101, 104, 107, 113 n.77
Ark, 21
Arṣy, 74, 88 n.8, 113 n.76
Asherah, 75
Ashtar-Chemosh, 35 n.46
Ashtaroth, 27, 35 n.47
Astarte, 27, 96
Astral worship, 36 n.53, 98
Athirat, 75, 77, 79, 107-8
Athtar, 98, 110 n.26

Baal, Aliyan (the Victor), 35 n.47, 51, 55-57, 67 n.1, 75, 95-97, 100; Berith, 27-29; as Fertility God, 51, 63, 93-103; Gad, 27; God of Ṣapon, 58; Hadad, 73; Judge, 56; Kanap, 35 n.47; Meon, 27, 35 n.46; of Peor, 24-26; Prince, Lord of the Earth, 33 n.21, 56, 97, 100; Rider of the Clouds, 56, 74-75, 95-96; Ṣapon, 35 n.47; Son of Dagon, 52-53, 79, 99; Storm God, 73-75; Tamar, 27; Zebul, 35 n.47; Zephon, 20, 34 n.29
Balaam, 40, 43, 45
Bathan, 65
Bel Anath, 27
Beth Dagon, 27; Peor, 24-26, 104; Shemesh, 27
Bull motif, 20-23, 29, 33 n.27, 34 n.30, 49 n.23, 96

Chaos, 53, 55, 57
Chemosh, 35 n.46
Cherubim, 21, 83
Circumcision, 28
Conflict motif, 13-31, 115-18, *et passim*
Cosmic forces, 30, 40-41, 54, 63, 66, 68 n.15, 115-18
Covenant Code, 15, 31 n.7, 35 n.37
Covenant, faith, 13-31, 43, 64, 115-18; formulations (treaty), 15, 19, 25, 28, 31 n.1, 32 n.9-10, 32 n.19, 45, 63; renewal, 20-26, 35 n.39; of Shechem, 27-31; of Sinai, 15-23, 26, 30
Creator, 42, 44, 49 n.22, 57
Creative activities, 44, 55, 57, 65-66, 70 n.49, 106, 110 n.31
Cult prostitution, 24, 35 n.44

Decalogue, 15, 26, 31 n.6
Dragon (monster), 54, 56, 65, 68 n.31, 95
Drought (aridity), 101-3

Egypt, 17, 29, 32 n.15, 33 n.22, 59, 65
Egyptian gods, 14-15, 34 n.29, 59
El, 41, 53-54, 67 n.5, 68 n.26, 75-76, 78-79, 83-84, 87, 91 n.56, 94, 99, 101-2; *'ab 'adam* (Father), 44, 97, 107; Berit, 28; as Bull, 34 n.30, 90 n.39; creator, 41-42, 99; Elyon, 41-42, 48 n.15; Lutpan (One of Heart), 90 n.39, 97, 99; Shaddai, 41
Election, 19, 29, 41-46, 49 n.20, 49 n.25, 63, 81, 87, 116
Eli, 41, 48 n.14
Elijah, 103, 111 n.46

Elyon, 41, 42, 44, 48 n.14
Enlil, 33 n.21
Exaltation (of the deity), 55-58, 60-62
Exodus, 14-15, 21, 26, 28, 43, 62-65, 70 n.56

Fertility, 55, 88 n.10, 93-111, 117-18; rites, 22, 25, 35 n.38, 98-100, 104-6, 109, 117-18
Festivals, 22, 35 n.37-39, 104, 112 n.55-56
Firstfruits, 99, 104-5
Formidable foe, 17, 32 n.15, 40, 53, 58-59, 65

Golden calf, 20-21, 26, 29, 33 n.27, 35 n.40, 35 n.43, 104
Grace, 16-18, 22, 29, 44
Habiru, 14
Hamor, 27
Hand (of God), 53, 60, 62, 77, 82
Heavenly attendants, 74, 82, 95
Heavenly council (holy ones), 30, 48 n.17, 52, 64, 69 n.46, 74-75, 83, 85-87, 91 n.49
Hieros gamos, 55, 57
Historical involvement, 16-19, 30, 41-42, 59-60, 63, 88, 108, 116ff
Hittite treaties, 17, 28, 32 n.9
Holy war, 27, 36 n.57
Humiliation (annihilation) of foe, 14, 16, 18, 33 n.22, 41, 54, 58, 60, 62, 68 n.17, 91 n.49

Idolatry (images), 21-23, 45, 101
Incomparable One, 56, 58, 60
Israel, as elect people, 19, 26, 30, 42, 44, 45, 87; as creation, 43-46, 60

Jealousy, 14, 16-18, 26-27, 30, 31 n.4, 35 n.42, 44-47, 63, 101-2, 109, 115-16
Jeroboam, 20-21, 33 n.27, 34 n.28
Jeshurun, 46, 82
Jethro, 15
Joshua, 17, 27-31
Judge River, 53-54, 56

Kathir and Khasis, 53-54
Keret, 79
Kinship, of Baal, 52-54, 58, 77-78; won by combat, 54, 62, 64; of Yahweh, 15, 26, 40-41, 45, 58-67, 86-88, 108, 115-16

Leviathan, 65-66, 68 n.31, 94, 118

Magnalia (mighty acts), 17-18, 26, 29, 40, 46, 60, 63, 88, 115-16
Marduk, 53, 65
Mari, 28, 70 n.50
Monotheism (monolatry), 16-17, 30, 46, 81
Mortuary rites, 97-98, 105-6
Moses, 21, 25
Mot, 62, 76, 93-96, 98-100, 102, 104, 109 n.3, 118
Mountain (holy), 58, 61-63, 70 n.52, 82
Murmur motif, 15, 31 n.6
Myth, 17, 19, 52, 63, 79, 116-17
Myth-ritual, 52, 79, 90 n.34-35

Nahar, 82
Name, 86
Nanna, 48 n.24
Nature, 63, 74-75, 95, 99, 101-3, 116-17
New Year Festival, 79, 89 n.16, 101
North, 31 n.2, 63, 74, 79

Pdry, 74
Plagues, 14-15
Poetic traditions, 39-49

Rahab, 65-66, 70 n.59, 83-84
Raḥam, 108
Rehoboam, 36 n.63
Reshep, 36 n.52, 40, 82, 91 n.47
Revivification, 98-101, 106
Ritual decalogue, 23, 104
Rock, 48 n.10, 108

Sacrifices, 23, 25, 36 n.48, 79, 90 n.29, 105
Ṣapon, 14, 30, 58, 98
Shapash, 94, 98-99
Shechem, 27-31, 36 n.63, 115-16
Sheol, 101
South, 13-14, 45, 80
Sovereignty, 18-19, 21-22, 40-44, 79-80, 83, 87-88, 102, 106, 115-16
Storm, 57, 60, 67, 73-75, 77, 80-81, 86-88, 89 n.36, 107

Tannin, 56, 64-66, 68 n.31
Temple, 57, 62, 75-79, 84-87, 89 n.17, 89 n.28
Terror, 45, 49 n.28, 56, 58, 61
Theophany, 14, 40, 45, 76, 80-91, 117
Tiamat, 53, 65
Ṭly, 74, 88 n.8

Underworld, 70 n.47, 93-97

Voice, 40, 77, 86-87, 91 n.58

Warrior God, 29, 40-41, 43, 46, 58-62, 64, 117
Waters, 53, 66, 101, 111 n.36
Windows, 76-77, 87, 89 n.21, 89 n.28, 102
Witness motif, 16-18, 26, 28, 30, 32 n.14
Wrath, 45-46, 82, 101-2

Yahweh, God of Israel, 27, 28, 45, 80, 82; as Father, 44, 46, 49 n.24; One of Sinai, 13, 45, 79, 82, 90 n.39, 108; Rider of the Clouds, 81, 82, 90 n.44
Yarikh, 108, 113 n.76
Yam, 53-54, 57, 60, 63, 65-66, 71 n.64, 74-75, 82-83, 118

www.ingramcontent.com/pod-product-compliance
Lightning Source LLC
Chambersburg PA
CBHW070459090426
42735CB00012B/2616
* 9 7 8 1 5 3 2 6 6 2 7 7 5 *